You

You

Amy Welborn

Our Sunday Visitor Publishing Division
Our Sunday Visitor, Inc.
Huntington, Indiana 46750

Nihil Obstat
Rev. Michael Heintz
Censor Librorum

Imprimatur
✠ John M. D'Arcy
Bishop of Fort Wayne-South Bend
July 3, 2007

The *Nihil Obstat* and *Imprimatur* are official declarations that a book is free from doctrinal or moral error. It is not implied that those who have granted the *Nihil Obstat* and *Imprimatur* agree with the contents, opinions, or statements expressed.

Our Sunday Visitor Publishing Division
Our Sunday Visitor, Inc.
200 Noll Plaza
Huntington, IN 46750

ISBN: 978-1-59276-319-1 (Inventory No. T418)
LCCN: 2007930710

Cover design: Amanda Miller
Cover photo: Shutterstock
Interior design: Sherri L. Hoffman
Interior illustrations: Andy Kurzen

PRINTED IN THE UNITED STATES OF AMERICA

Contents

As Jesus passed on from there, he saw a man called Matthew sitting at the tax office; and he said to him, "Follow me." And he rose and followed him.

— Matthew 9:9

God, you have made us for yourself, and our hearts are restless till they find their rest in you.

— St. Augustine, *Confessions*

I know that you as young people have great aspirations, that you want to pledge yourselves to build a better world. Let others see this, let the world see it, since this is exactly the witness that the world expects from the disciples of Jesus Christ; in this way, and through your love above all, the world will be able to discover the star that we follow as believers.

— Pope Benedict XVI, Homily, World Youth Day, Cologne, Germany, August 21, 2005

CHAPTER 1

Who Am I?

WHO ARE YOU?

No, no, no. Don't just rattle off your name, birthday, and address and turn the page.

Because . . . would that be . . . you?

I'll say it again: Who . . . are . . . you?

That's a big question.

Let's start answering it by thinking through your day, from the time you grudgingly open those eyes to the moment you gratefully close them again. Who is that person, anyway? Who's that person called "you"?

An exhausted slug who doesn't want to get out of bed for various reasons, including that Algebra test?

A consumer of clothes and breakfast?

A student of various kinds. World History = Great Student. Algebra = Not.

A friend?

An enemy? Harsh, but true.

A comedian? A good listener? A ringleader?

A consumer of snacks and lunch?

An athlete, a musician, an actor, an artist, a burger-flipper, a salesperson?

A big brother, little sister?

Daughter, son?

A consumer of music, electronic stuff, and maybe a car?
An avatar?
A gamer?
A television-watcher?
A customer, a potential consumer, a market share?
One tired human being?

Which one? All of them? Probably, at some point in the day, you're all this and more.

So . . . who are you?

This book is about choices. It's about the life you're choosing to lead, not when you get older and your choices suddenly "matter," but right now, because your choices matter *now*. Good choices, bad choices, neutral choices. It's about what you're going to make of the short time you've got on this earth with the gifts you've been given.

And trust me — you *do* have gifts. Lots of them.

So it makes sense to start with the question of who is this "you" we're talking about. If you don't have a clear, bottom-line sense of who you are, you're at great risk for being swept in all kinds of weird and destructive directions by forces that want to use and exploit whatever part of "you" they can get their hands on.

And not because those forces love you a lot and want the very best for you, either.

Did you notice how often "consumer" appeared on our list up there? Why did it? Well, maybe because it's worth thinking about how many of our choices are shaped by forces that want us to believe that buying their stuff will make us happy. And who's helped by that, in the end?

So . . . who are you?

You play all sorts of roles during the course of your day. But you know that not any single one of those roles really *is* you, totally and completely. Even the list of all of those roles can't define you. So what can?

If you think about it, the most important things in life can't be neatly defined or summed up in a paragraph. There's such a thing as mystery, and every human person is a wonderful, intriguing mystery.

Some more mysterious than others, you have to admit. But that's another chapter.

So sure, we're each a mystery. We even have a hard time understanding ourselves sometimes. But there *is* someone who gets it, who doesn't find you to be mysterious in the least.

That would be the One who created that mystery called "you" in the first place.

God.

Suppose you found a weird, wildly colored blob of a sculpture dropped at your doorstep one morning. What in the world? What would be the first question you'd ask?

Who did this? Why?

 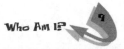

If you knew the answers to that, you might understand the meaning and purpose of the . . . er . . . gift a little better.

Same with us. Because we're sort of weird, wildly colored blobs, too. *Very* mysterious.

If we want to dive into that mystery, to get who we really are, the best place to start is to remember where we came from — or who we came from. It makes no sense to start anywhere else. So let's start here:

Your existence here on this planet, at this moment, to put it bluntly, is no accident.

Oh, sure, people may say that you're nothing but an accident — even your parents, but the fact is, even if your biological parents didn't intend to create you at the moment you were created, God worked through their actions, through that meeting of sperm and egg to create someone very, very specific — you.

On purpose. Because God wanted you to exist, to live, to hope, to dream, to help, to love, to be.

There's your beginning. That crucial truth to hold in your head and heart, to store up, to treasure, to reflect on, to hope on:

I'm here because God wants me to be here.

Wrap your head around that. Repeat daily. Twice, if necessary. It just might change how you think about yourself.

> For you have formed my inward parts, you knitted me together in my mother's womb. I praise you, for I am wonderfully made.
> — Psalm 139:13-14

So . . . you might be thinking . . . what's that got to do with choices? With right and wrong? With this whole book, for Pete's sake?

Everything. And here's why:

Your belief about who you are shapes your decisions.

So, if you believe that you're basically useless and a burden to others . . . your decisions are probably not going to be based in a sense of hope in what you have to offer the world.

If you believe that you're bad, you might not even bother to try to do good.

If you believe that you're an accident of nature who's essentially all alone in the universe, you might be prone to thinking that the only view of life that matters is the one in your own head. Who cares what the other accidents of nature think, anyway?

There's something else, as well. It's not just about who you think you are, but who you think *other human beings* are, as well.

You could probably predict that a person who believes life is an accident and that we're all on our own might make different choices about how to treat other people than a person who believes that every person they meet is a beloved child of God, right?

That's why in this book about life, choices, and what it all leads to, we're starting with that question of who you are.

If you passionately and deeply believe that God created you and every single other person on purpose because He loves them and wants them to exist and know happiness and love . . . how are you going to act?

How are you going to use your time?

What kind of future are you going to work for?

How are you going to treat your own body?

How are you going to talk to others? How are you going to talk about them?

What's your relationship to the truth going to be?

How are you going to interact with others?

How are you going to treat their opinions, their dreams and their bodies?

How are you going to think about and treat the unborn, little children, the elderly, poor, the sick and the helpless?

How are you going to think about how you make money and why you make money?

Finally — and maybe most importantly — when you are making all of these decisions — *whose voice* are you going to be guided by? Who are you going to listen to?

Who knows best what's good for you, for others, and for the world?

The One who made the whole thing, maybe?

Maybe?

> We exist because God is good.
>
> — St. Augustine,
> De Doctrina Christiana, 1.31

So ... What Now?

IT'S EASY FOR US to say, "Yeah, yeah. God made me, God knows what's best for me, yeah, God's first. I always listen to Him most of all. Sure."

But do we? Or do we just say it, and go on our merry way, listening to all sorts of voices *except* God's?

That's the challenge we face, and it's a huge one. It's the challenge of the human race, going back to the very beginning. And speaking of the beginning:

In the beginning . . .

Let's look at what happened there, in this story that reflects the deepest truths about who we are.

Adam and Eve, given all they could want or need by the God who made and loved them, decided, quite simply, that they knew better.

The "Tree of Knowledge of Good and Evil" is a sort of mysterious thing, but in essence it represents the power to *determine* what

is good and evil, right and wrong, what is good for us and leads to our happiness, and what leads to misery and death.

Only God has that power. We don't.

Adam and Eve picked some fruit. Forbidden Fruit, we call it — but why was it forbidden? Because God doesn't want us to enjoy ourselves, who wants to keep us in some sort of childish state of dependency?

No.

Because it's reality. The world was created and structured in a certain way by God. It wasn't you, me, or a distant crabby ancestor who decided that honesty was good or selfishness was bad.

In fact, if it were up to *us*... those values probably definitely wouldn't be set in stone, would they?

(Honestly, now.)

Right and wrong are built into the texture of the universe and even into our own selves — that thing called conscience. You know it. You also know that you expect other people to know it and probably get sort of upset when they act like they don't. Especially if it hurts *you*.

God made it this way. Why? Because He made everything *good* and for a purpose, lovingly building in the map on how to reach that destination into His creation.

One of those creations being you.

So back to Adam and Eve. What happens when they ditch God and grasp that power to determine right and wrong for themselves?

Several things:

- They realize that they are "naked." That is, their bodies become a source of shame.
- They immediately start blaming each other for the problem.
- They hide from God.
- They must leave the Garden.

It's amazingly easy to see how this dynamic works in our own lives today. What happens to you when you do something wrong? Dishonesty creeps into your life. You blame others, or just life and fate, for what you did. You're not sure who you are anymore. You feel distant from your true self. Maybe you pray less because you're ashamed and you don't want to face God.

So there you have it: choices and you. Your choices can take you in one of two directions: Either closer to who you really are, or further away.

How can you tell which choice will take you where?

How can you figure out which voice you should listen to?

How can you be . . . you?

"Are not two sparrows sold for a penny? And not one of them will fall to the ground without your Father's will. But even the hairs of your head are all numbered. Fear not, therefore; you are of more value than many sparrows."

— Matthew 10:29-31

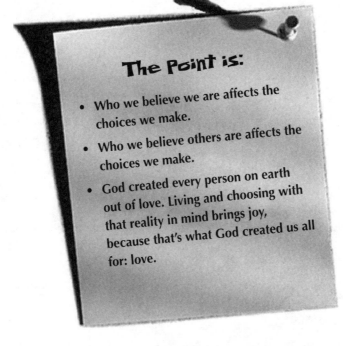

The Point is:

- Who we believe we are affects the choices we make.
- Who we believe others are affects the choices we make.
- God created every person on earth out of love. Living and choosing with that reality in mind brings joy, because that's what God created us all for: love.

CHAPTER 2

Sure I Want to Be a Good Person. But . . . How?

"BE GOOD!"

How many times have you heard that? Too many to count, probably, from the time you were very small.

It's the first glimmer we get of right and wrong: those moments in which our little child selves glowed in the praise of being "good" and stung from the accusation that we'd been "bad." And maybe even literally *stung*. Ouch.

Weirdly, though, over the years, meanings get reversed. We get into that stage in life in which we cringe if we're told that we're good, and actually feel sort of proud about being known as kind of edgy, dark and, well . . . *bad*.

Some of that probably comes from the fact that in the land you're living in — the land of teens — stuff that's "bad" is often stuff that's simply about venturing into the adult world: acting as if adults can't have authority over you, drinking, sexual activity, breaking rules that seem to be about keeping you a child. "Good" teens cooperate with the prison guards. "Bad" ones want to break out.

Thinking of it that way, who'd want to be good?

There must be a better way to think about "good" and "bad" — a way that isn't tied to what your peers think or how old you are. A more objective way, maybe?

We'll be talking about good and bad choices for the next hundred pages or so. How can we tell the difference in a way that sticks, in a way that's real, in a way that's consistent and makes sense for us whether we're 15 or 51?

Not a new problem. Ever since human beings noticed that some actions and attitudes brought more harm than help, philosophers have pondered that question. What is good? How can we best seek, find and live the good?

> **For I do not do the good I want, but the evil I do not want is what I do.**
>
> — Romans 7:19

It might help, too, to understand that this is not just a problem for Catholics or religious freaks in general. If you read ancient pagan philosophers, you'll find them grappling with it. If you examine the writings of Hindu, Buddhist, and Muslim thinkers, it's there.

Defining Some Terms

Morality: "Referring to the goodness or evil of human acts."
— *Catechism of the Catholic Church*, glossary

Conscience: "Deep within his conscience man discovers a law which he has not laid upon himself but which he must obey. Its voice, ever calling him to love and to do what is good and to avoid evil, sounds in his heart at the right moment.... For man has in his heart a law inscribed by God.... His conscience is man's most secret core and his sanctuary. There he is alone with God whose voice echoes in his depths." — *Catechism of the Catholic Church*, 1776, from *Gaudium et spes*, 16

Which should tell you something important, something to learn right now and never forget:

This whole business of goodness isn't just something invented to personally torment *you*. It's not about violating random rules written by people who just don't get what life today is like.

No. If you take a look at how people have thought about moral goodness through history, across cultures, you'll see pretty broad agreement as to what characterizes a "good person": integrity, honesty, respect, kindness, faithfulness, non-attachment to possessions, selflessness.

Put it this way: Look as hard as you want but you're not going to find a religious system in the world that is going to tell you that lying to your parents or using another person for your own benefit or pleasure helps you grow into being a good person.

Being Good

IN CATHOLIC LINGO, over thousands of years we've defined some concepts that are basic to the idea of goodness: the virtues.

???

"VIRTUE" SOUNDS OLD-FASHIONED, from a world of horses and buggies, curtsies and calling-cards.

It's not, though. "Virtue" is a good word, a word that gets across that notion of goodness without making you feel like a little kid or giving you the idea that it's all about rules.

In fact, "living a virtuous life" has a fairly mature ring to it. It sounds as if someone's going somewhere and doing something important and meaningful. Which is a good goal to shoot for, don't you think?

> It is no great thing to live long, nor even to live for ever; but it is a great thing to live well.
> — St. Augustine, *Sermons*, 127.2

So what are the virtues? Let's do a quick run-through.

???

IN CATHOLIC THINKING, a virtue is an attitude, stance, and habit (which means you *do it*, not just *think it*) that is going to lead you to God, lead you to being the best person you can be, the person God *created* you to be.

That's what human life is about. It's about being the best human beings we can be, fulfilling our God-given goals and destinies. What takes us closer to being the people God made us to be = moral. What takes us further away = immoral.

Virtues are the habits that help us choose morally.

The virtues are grouped into two categories: those we can only find through God's grace, and those we can find and build up ourselves (although grace doesn't hurt there, either!).

Theological Virtues

Faith

Your first attempt to define faith might simply be "believing in God."

Well, true. But there's more because, you know, even the devil believes that God exists.

Hmmm. Yet even more food for thought.

Faith is more than just head-belief, although that's a part of it. The virtue of faith is believing that God is God.

Huh?

Well . . . think about it. If God is God (all-powerful, all-knowing, all-loving Creator of you) . . . then who should be in charge of your life?

Maybe . . . God?

So that's what faith is. It's a way of life in which you live, in a very practical way, with the trust that God is in charge. He's your only real judge. He sets the standards for your life. He's the one you listen to about *everything*. He's your best friend.

That's faith.

> Faith is believing that God believes in you.
> — Andre Dubus, *A Father's Story*

Hope

Hope definitely gets a bad rap. People tend to associate "hope" with being out of touch, with being a dreamer.

How is living in a fantasy a virtue?

It's not. And that's not what the *virtue* of hope is, either.

Hope is trust that God is in charge and that He wants the best for us and, finally, that God's goodness will eventually win out. If you want to visualize "hope," take a look at that crucifix. Again.

> Paul, an apostle of Christ Jesus by command
> of God our Savior and of Christ Jesus our
> hope...
>
> — 1 Timothy 1:1

(*Revelation* — the last book in the Bible — is pretty much Hope 101. Read it.)

You might be seeing a connection here, by the way. If you don't have even a little bit of the virtue of faith, hope might be hard to come by.

But why is hope a virtue?

Well, think about being, well... good. Or virtuous. Doing the right thing.

Is it easy?

Probably not. Doing the right thing often means being rejected, or at the very least mocked and labeled in some weird way.

It takes a lot of hope to get through that and keep walking.

You can really only do it if you've opened your heart to the virtue of hope. If you trust that no matter what those bozos say, Jesus is right, you *shouldn't* exclude that new kid or make life rotten for a teacher. You have to breathe deeply, trust Jesus and *not* the bozos and you have to... hope.

Sins Against Hope

Watch out for these:

Despair: Losing all hope in God and yourself as God's beloved child.

Presumption: Too much of the wrong kind of hope. Believing that you don't have to try to do the right thing or be a good person — that God will excuse anything.

Hope is a virtue.

Charity

Charity is love, plain and simple. It's love for God, first, and then love for others, just like Jesus says:

> "Teacher, which is the great commandment in the law?" And he said to him, "You shall love the Lord your God with all your heart, and with all your soul, and with all your mind. This is the great and first commandment. And a second is like it, You shall love your neighbor as yourself." (MATTHEW 22:36-39)

So there you go. Not optional, not if you feel like it, not if it will get you what you want.

A *commandment.*

We're going to be coming back to the concept of — and the *commandment* to — love quite a bit in this book because it's sort of basic to questions of morality. Obviously. But for now just get this:

The virtue of charity involves devotion to God, and an attitude of gratitude to God. It starts right there: with God. Why do we love?

> God is love, and he who abides in love abides in God, and God abides in him. In this is love perfected with us, that we may have confidence for the day of judgment, because as he is so are we in this world. There is no fear in love, but perfect love casts out fear. For fear has to do with punishment, and he who fears is not perfected in love. We love, because he first loved us. (1 JOHN 4:16-19)

There you go. We love — as Jesus *commanded* — because God loved us. Love — real love — must be shared. We love others because . . . God loves *them.*

It's about seeing every single person, as best we can, the way God sees them.

And since God loves everyone . . . we do, too.

What does that mean?

I've always found it helpful to think of it this way:

When I love, I commit myself to seeing that other person as God sees him or her: as a beloved child, for whom He wants happiness and joy. God doesn't want His children to be miserable: neither do I, and how dreadful would it be for me to actually cause unhappiness like that.

God doesn't want harm to come to His children, and neither do I.

Now practicing this virtue isn't always sweetness and light. It's hard, hard, hard — which is why it's one of those "theological virtues" that really only comes from God's grace.

It's hard because, well, it's hard to love difficult people, people who have hurt you.

It's also hard in a different way, because sometimes love involves, not kisses and hugs, but truth telling and honesty.

You know how your parents always say, "I'm doing this because I love you"?

Well, they're right.

Think about it. If your friend was all giddy and in love with some guy who everyone could see was mistreating her . . . would it be "loving" to just nod and go along with her fantasy? Or would a really charity-filled thing to do be to tell her the truth about what she's not seeing, no matter what the risk to your friendship?

Yeah. Love — the virtue of charity — is hard.

> "This is my commandment, that you love one another as I have loved you. Greater love has no man than this, that a man lay down his life for his friends."
>
> — John 15:12-13

Ask Jesus.

You know — up there on that cross?

There are four other basic virtues, which are called "Cardinal." These are more natural virtues that we know about naturally, and which people can develop even if they don't know God. Although, as with everything else . . . knowing God helps. A lot.

Prudence

The virtue of prudence is about taking stock and being careful.

You can probably identify with this one.

Remember the times you've spoken (or yelled) before you've done any thinking?

Or the times you've let your emotions be in charge? Or the times you've been swept up into a sort of tidal wave of idiocy along with your friends?

Not very prudent.

If you're going to be a virtuous or good person, you have to develop this virtue called prudence. It means that every time you've got a decision to make that's either going to take you closer to the good or further away, you make yourself stop, breathe, and go through some steps:

⤷ You think and consult other smart people.

⤷ You look honestly and objectively at the situation.

⤷ You really resolve to act on what's right.

Justice

Justice is pretty easy to understand because we have this tendency to really value it when it comes to our own lives.

Not quite sure what I mean? Well, just think. . .

"That's not *fair*!"

Yeah. How many times have you said or thought that in your life?

The trick of justice as a virtue, though, is to widen that circle, not just a little bit, but a lot.

Are you the only person in the world who deserves to be treated fairly?

Not quite. So the virtue of justice involves being committed to the truth that everyone deserves their "rightful due."

And it involves *living* that way. So you know . . . is it *just* that your parents should have to pick up after you all the time? Is it *just* that a teacher should have to put up with a bunch of nonsense from her students when she's just trying to do her job? Is it *just*. . .

Widen the circle a little bit more . . . is it *just* that lots and lots of people in the world don't have clean water or enough food to eat when others have all they want and complain that they can't have even more empty calories to consume?

Temperance

Temperance is kind of a fun virtue (really!), because it hits close to home for most of us. The virtue of temperance is basically moderation: you know when enough is enough and too much is too much.

This is obviously common sense, but there's a deeper spiritual dimension to temperance that touches on our relationship with God and His creation.

When we practice the virtue of temperance, we're saying that we're grateful to God for the gifts He's given that bring us pleasure — but we know the proper place for those gifts. We're not letting them take over our lives. We're not letting them distract us from the good we've been put here on earth to do. We're not letting them be in control of our lives . . . we're not confusing them with God.

If you think about it, taking the virtue of temperance seriously might make a difference in a lot of areas in your life:

- How much you eat and drink, naturally.
- How much time you spend gaming.
- How much time you spend on the Internet.
- How much time you spend watching television.
- How much time you spend texting.
- How much time you spend just "hanging out."

Temperance can also come in handy when we get older and are faced with different temptations. For example, if someone's working 60 hours a week, not because they need the money, but because they are craving success and power, and their family is suffering . . . temperance, maybe?

???

TEMPERANCE ISN'T ABOUT not enjoying yourself. Not at all. The Christian life is supposed to be joyful, enjoying the good things God has given us, but in a balanced way that takes us closer to that goal.

Did God *really* create you to sit on a couch all day gaming and chatting, with junk food dribbling down the front of your shirt?

Maybe . . . not.

> No one is really happy merely because he has what he wants, but only if he wants things he ought to want.
> — St. Augustine, in Ps 26, *Enarr*, 2.7

Fortitude

Fortitude isn't hard to understand. Obviously, it's strength — but a little more.

The virtue of fortitude isn't stubbornness or willfulness just for its own sake. No, this virtue is about firmness of spirit — a commitment to doing the right thing, to following God's desires for you, no matter what the obstacles.

This is easier for some people than others, and that's the interesting thing about all of these virtues in general. Not all of them might be a big challenge for every person. There are some people who are naturally temperate, for example, who don't have any huge desire to overindulge in anything. Others are naturally prudent — sometimes a bit too prudent, when it comes to the point of not being able to make a decision at all.

And there are some folks who are gifted with a natural dose of fortitude, who seem to almost effortlessly stand up for what they believe, who just *don't care* about other people's opinions.

Is that you? Maybe — or maybe not.

If not, then you're going to have to work on it, to build it up.

Start with little things — fighting a small temptation to be mean to someone or avoid a responsibility. Pray, breathe, and gather up just a *little bit* more strength — fortitude — to do what you know is right.

And after a time, you might find that when the time comes to fight big temptations, you've got it — fortitude.

> I know how to be abased, and I know how to abound; in any and all circumstances I have learned the secret of facing plenty and hunger, abundance and want. I can do all things in him who strengthens me.
>
> — Philippians 4:12-13

So there you go. The building blocks to goodness, to being a great person, the person you were created to be, the person who's going to bring the most joy to others in this world.

Just remember — and this is *so, so* important — that none of this is automatic. Virtues are *habits*.

There is really nothing in life that we're born knowing how to do (except cry and . . . er . . . other things). We have to learn *everything* — from how to get the spoon from the bowl to our mouths, to riding a bike to balancing chemical equations to putting up a good soccer defense.

And we only learn those things — become an expert eater, biker, chemist, athlete — by practicing. Starting in small blocks, and building up to bigger skills. You can't write a poem until you know how to make your letters. You can't play Beethoven without learning the scales. You can't be a really good athlete without drills, drills, drills.

The same applies to the virtues — all of them individually and together.

You and I were born with the potential to be virtuous people. We were born with the potential to be saints!

But it doesn't happen automatically. It doesn't even come naturally to some of us. We have lots of obstacles to overcome.

But bit by bit . . . step by step . . . we take baby steps, and before long, who knows?

We might just be running.

> Lord, teach me to be generous.
> Teach me to serve you as you deserve;
> to give and not to count the cost,
> to fight and not to heed the wounds,
> to toil and not to seek for rest,
> to labor and not to ask for reward,
> save that of knowing that I do your will.
> — St. Ignatius of Loyola

The Point is:

- The desire to be a good person is planted in human beings by God. The knowledge of what that means is, too. It's universal.

- The virtues are essential in helping us grow into the joyful, loving people God created us to be.

CHAPTER 3

LET'S SEE where we are:

> You = beloved child of God, created for a purpose.
>
> Others = ditto.
>
> Living out God's purpose for your life: Virtues help. A lot.

We've seen a few other things, too. That purpose God made you for isn't misery, self-hate, and inaction. It's a deep inner joy that comes from living in the certainty of God's love.

We've also hinted that the whole idea of identifying virtue with your wholeness and happiness isn't a rules thing. It's not a Christian thing, even. It's a *human* thing.

Take a look:

From the Koran:

> Those who act kindly in this world will have kindness.
>
> — KORAN, 39:10

From a Buddhist scripture:

> Make haste in doing good; check your mind from evil.
>
> — DHAMMAPADA, 116

From Hinduism:

What sort of religion can it be without compassion? You need to show compassion to all living beings.

— BASAVANNA, VACANA, 247

From the Jewish Talmud:

All men are responsible for one another.

— SANHEDRIN, 27b

From Confucius:

The man of perfect virtue, wishing to be established himself, seeks also to establish others; wishing to be enlarged himself, he seeks also to enlarge others.

— ANALECTS, 6:28.2

THE KNOWLEDGE OF what brings the greatest happiness to each person and the whole world is a *natural* knowledge. God plants it in every human heart: Paul, writing in his letter to the Romans, says exactly that:

When Gentiles who have not the law do by nature what the law requires, they are a law to themselves, even though they do not have the law. They show that what the law requires is written on their hearts, while their conscience also bears witness... (ROMANS 2:14-15A)

So what does that mean?

It means, most of all, that the big leap we have to take from a child's view of morality to an adult's view is recognizing that the "rules" we've been taught reflect the deeper reality of the way all

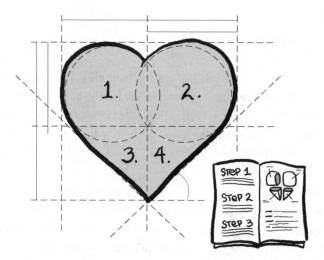

human beings are called to treat one another . . . just because we're human.

God made us, and included in the package are . . . directions.

So . . . is that it?

No, that's not it. The virtues are an excellent place to start, and good, virtuous people live in every culture, at every time, and follow different religions and the natural law of morality God has planted in their hearts. You can't argue with that.

But there's more. Let's dig and find it.

SEE, HERE'S THE THING:

What happens when you do something wrong?

Is that the end of it? We certainly hope so, don't we? Like Adam and Eve, we try to just blow it off, to refuse responsibility, to shrug and talk about "mistakes," or "too bad that happened," hoping that will be the end of it.

But it's not.

The consequences of sin just keep giving and giving. Isn't sin great that way?

Dipping back into Genesis, we see that, clearly and painfully. Because, if you recall, after Adam and Eve left the garden, alienated from God and their true selves . . . that wasn't the end of it for them. They had a son, Cain, who got angry and jealous of his brother, Abel, and murdered him (Genesis 4).

Sin separates us from one another.

And then, if you remember, there's another major event — more and more people are born, live, and die, and these people do worse and worse things, until God is so disappointed in what His creatures have done with their freedom, He decides to start over again. A flood, an ark, a rainbow (Genesis 6-8).

A tough story, but true: Sin spreads, infects the whole world, and results in our destruction.

Take a look at the newspapers. Flip through your history book and consider just the twentieth century and even these first few years of the twenty-first. Is this really the creation God intended? Is this mess of mass destruction, selfishness, bigotry, horrible wars, and genocide really what your innermost self — that God-given con-science — tells you the way it's all supposed to be?

When the wrong choices are made . . . is that the end of it? Is everything — including our inner selves, including the whole world — just . . . *okay*?

Go back to those newspapers. Think about your inner life. It's a mess for sure. It's broken.

We're broken. We do something God didn't create us to do: we die.

But . . . *God so loved the world.* . . .

IN THE CHRISTIAN VOCABULARY, these "mistakes" have a name: sin, and it might be a good idea to try to recover that word. If someone steals your stuff, does their "Oh, wow, sorry I made a mistake and did that . . . everyone makes mistakes" really cover it?

Nope. Sin, which comes from a Hebrew word that means "miss the mark," is a word we need to let back into our vocabulary. We *sin*. We miss the mark of what God wants for us, hopes for us, made us for.

The consequences of sin — yours, mine, and ours — is a broken world.

The consequences of sin — yours, mine, and ours — is suffering and death.

The consequences of sin — yours, mine, and ours — is this feeling that things *just aren't the way they're supposed to be.*

> I consider that the sufferings of this present time are not worth comparing with the glory that is to be revealed to us. For the creation waits with eager longing for the revealing of the sons of God; for the creation was subjected to futility, not of its own will but by the will of him who subjected it in hope; because the creation itself will be set free from its bondage to decay and obtain the glorious liberty of the children of God. We know that the whole creation has been groaning with labor pains until now.
>
> — Romans 8:18-22

But . . . what can we do?

God made us for better things. God made us in His image, to live with Him forever.

How can we, poor sinners, manage this? We can't get up in the morning and get out of the house without messing up. Our lives feel broken because of the sins of our parents. We're sort of sad and hopeless, carrying around this burden, wondering how we can be forgiven — *really* forgiven in a real, lasting way that brings us a kind of rebirth.

JESUS.

Jesus, God made flesh, came into the world — the whole world, your life and mine — to re-create, to redeem, to fix, to reconcile.

In Jesus we see something really important, something that might change our lives, if we watch and listen carefully:

- In Jesus, God comes into the world to do what only God can do: conquer sin and death.
- In Jesus, God comes into the world to do what a human being *had* to do: take on the guilt for the sins of the world.
- In Jesus' sacrifice, the world is re-created. That is the "power of the Cross."
- So for us: When we turn to Jesus, our sins are *forgiven*. I can forgive you for what you did to me, but can my forgiveness "fix" your sin? Can my words forgive you in the core of the being that's done the wrong thing?

As you can see, the virtues get us going and can help us be excellent people, but when it comes to saintliness — there's more.

Saints are motivated by a bit more than the desire to be virtuous. Saints are motivated by *passion*.

Here is what the saints see: they see suffering. They see that the most profound suffering is connected, in one way or another, every time, to sin: we suffer either because we're leading sinful lives and

are bearing the consequences, or we're suffering because we're suffering the consequences of someone else's sins of greed, anger, selfishness, or a million other things that are the opposite of virtues.

Saints are motivated to meet the suffering, to reach out and into the suffering, to heal the suffering.

Saints are motivated because they've met someone who has healed their suffering, bound up *their* wounds, suffers with them and rises to glory: Jesus.

Saints are motivated to follow Jesus, to walk with Him and even more deeply — to let Him live in them and meet the suffering of this world through *them.*

Saints bravely and realistically confront the suffering in their own souls, in their neighbor, in the world and, nourished by Jesus, let Him love through them, knowing that completely joined to the living Jesus, they'll be joined to Him forever, in joy, where there is not a bit of suffering at all.

> It seemed to him at that moment, that it would have been quite easy to have been a saint. It would only have needed a little self-restraint and a little courage. He felt like someone who had missed happiness by seconds at an appointed place. He knew now that at the end there was only one thing that counted — to be a saint.
>
> — Graham Greene,
> *The Power and the Glory* (emphasis mine)

The name of this book is "Prove It! You."

That's not because we want you to be all vain and think that you're so fantastic you need a whole book singing your praises.

No, it's called "You" because it's about your choices, the choices you make to shape this life that God has given you.

So . . . before we get to the specific choices, let's make sure the stage is set.

- You . . . loved by God.
- You . . . created to be happy.
- You . . . given a conscience.
- You . . . living a virtuous life that will bring happiness.
- You . . . in a suffering world.
- You . . . part of the pierced, suffering, to-be-glorified Body of Christ.
- You . . . reaching out to Jesus.
- You . . . called to be a saint.

Sure, this book is called "Prove It! You," but did you notice who's on the cover?

Rise up . . . and follow me.

> They [saints] show us the way to attain happiness, they show us how to be truly human. Through all the ups and downs of history, they were the true reformers who constantly rescued it from plunging into the valley of darkness; it was they who constantly shed upon it the light that was needed to make sense — even in the midst of suffering — of God's words spoken at the end of the work of creation: "It is very good."
>
> — Pope Benedict XVI, Cologne, World Youth Day, August 2005

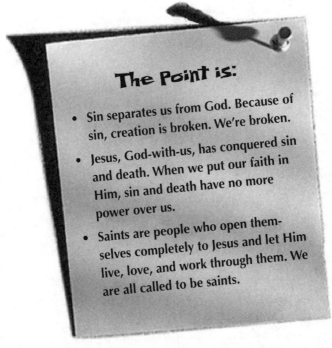

The Point is:

- Sin separates us from God. Because of sin, creation is broken. We're broken.

- Jesus, God-with-us, has conquered sin and death. When we put our faith in Him, sin and death have no more power over us.

- Saints are people who open themselves completely to Jesus and let Him live, love, and work through them. We are all called to be saints.

CHAPTER 4

It Was Only a Little Lie. So?

IT'S NIGHT. YOU'RE ONLINE. MySpace, Facebook, Friendster — whatever. There's messaging and chatting and all kinds of things going on.

In this world . . . who are you?

You've got a name . . . or two or three of them.

You've got pictures and interests and songs on your profile.

It's all there, it's busy and you're busy and there are people from all over the place in your world, talking back, posting comments . . . to you. You.

But . . . is it you?

Who are you there — online?

Are you telling the truth about who you are?

It's night again, and you've got a choice.

Tell the truth to your parents about where you're going and be locked in your room, or tell a lie and be free to go off with a wave?

Are you telling the truth about who you are?

Okay . . . one more time. Night — again.

You're on a date with someone who's okay, but not any great love of your life.

He wants to do more than you do, he wants and is willing to go further. You're not comfortable, it doesn't fit with how you feel, but. . .

You *really* want a boyfriend.

Or you *really* are feeling revved up.

Whatever you choose. . .

Are you telling the truth about who you are . . . your best self?

IN THIS BOOK about moral choices and you, we're not going to start the specifics with the usual, like sex and drinking and other exciting things. We're going to get even more basic than that and talk about a stance that underlies almost everything else we do, every choice:

Honesty.

And to be, well, honest, I'll also let you know that in my nine years of teaching in a Catholic high school, I was constantly struck by what a huge problem dishonesty was among my students. Oh sure, kids have always lied now and then, but what bothered me was how so many kids just sort of took it for granted that dishonesty — which includes lying and cheating — was just a way of life, and was okay.

Why was it okay?

Because, it seemed, the purpose of life was basically to get what you wanted: a decent grade, admission to the college you want, your homework turned in, a night out clubbing — and if you had to twist the truth to get it . . . oh well.

Who cares, anyway?

I don't want to use this chapter to give big lectures or run down specific scenarios of *why* lying is bad *here* and what your different *strategies* should be . . . and so on.

I'm sure you've done that enough in religion class or religious education.

What I want to do instead is challenge you and to shake up the way you think about the question of honesty.

It's not about getting what you want.

It's about being who you *are*.

All sin is a kind of lying.
— St. Augustine, *Against Lying*

Why be dishonest?

Think of the reasons people (okay . . . *you*) are dishonest at times. Why lie, either directly or indirectly?

(That last word was added because I've had loads of conversations with kids telling me that *not mentioning* to your parents that "going out with my friends" actually means "going to a club forty miles away and using a fake ID to get in and party and drink" isn't a lie because, you know . . . you have to use words to lie. No. You. Don't.)

Why?

← We're dishonest so we can stay out of trouble.

← We're dishonest so we can avoid embarrassment.

↳ We're dishonest so we can do the things we want to do and get the things we want.

↳ We're dishonest because we want to protect our friends.

Now look at the list, and ponder it. What ties all of these concerns, these motivations, together? What is it we seem dead set and determined to avoid?

Suffering, maybe?

I think so. Because being in trouble, embarrassed, separated from our friends, and seeing our friends get in trouble involve suffering. So do bad grades and having to work for the stuff we want instead of just taking it.

And you know what? That's not surprising. It's sort of natural. It would actually be sort of weird to *want* to suffer. It sort of makes sense when we're presented with Choice A, which will involve telling the truth but suffering, and Choice B, which will involve dishonesty but will get us what we want without the suffering we're trying to avoid.

Our instinct, quite a bit, is to choose B.

So — IS THERE A PROBLEM? What could it be?

Maybe. Think about the times you've lied and been dishonest in various ways.

Looking back . . . was there — when it was all said and done — No Suffering Involved?

Really?

No one suffered? *Ever?*

Yeah, thought so.

We're talking about honesty, but the fact is, here's something that's true for the moral — the *virtuous* — life in general:

You can't avoid suffering. You just can't.

And when you try to avoid suffering by making a sinful choice, you just end up pushing the suffering away from yourself, just for the moment.

You push it onto other people.

You're also pushing it back off onto yourself in the *future*. Do you remember how we said the virtuous life involves building habits — that virtues are actually habits?

So are their opposites — the vices. So sure, build that habit of lying to people you say you love.

How is that going to help you to become an honest person, exactly?

❓ ❓ ❓

BECAUSE, NO MATTER HOW you justify any lying that you do, and no matter how satisfied you are with the results, there is a part of you that . . . *knows*.

Knows that human beings shouldn't be lying to one another. That really, you can't build relationships of any kind on dishonesty. That lying takes its toll.

That God didn't go to all the trouble to create you just so you could lie about who you are.

> Therefore, putting away falsehood, let every-
> one speak the truth with his neighbors, for
> we are members one of another.
> — Ephesians 4:25

This is not an easy thing I'm talking about here. It's hard because you live in a world that is pressing on you with huge, impossible expectations, aren't you?

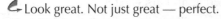

↳ Look great. Not just great — perfect.

↳ Achieve. Be the best. Make no mistakes — ever.

↳ Be really good at a whole lot of different things. They call it "well-rounded," but you might just call it "exhausted."

↳ But at the same time . . . not take things too seriously. Because it's all about being funny and sarcastic and not letting on that you feel much of anything.

You can probably add to that list the expectations your own personal family and circle of friends put on you.

No wonder we're tempted to dishonesty. Who can keep up? Who can meet all of those expectations? Of course, we have to lie to protect that image. Of course, we have to cheat — to copy other people's homework, to get essays from online instead of writing them ourselves, to never, ever read a book we're assigned. Of course, we have to pretend to be someone we're not to our parents so they won't punish us for what we're really doing, and, of course, we have to lie a little to our friends so they won't think we're lame.

What a mess we find ourselves in. What a prison.

Sometimes, people think of religious faith as confining, as a set of rules that were instituted for the sole reason of keeping us from being ourselves.

Well, that just doesn't mesh with reality, because when you actually sit down and study what the followers of Jesus say about their lives before and after, one of the things you'll hear one hundred percent of the time is that turning your life over to Jesus is an incredibly *freeing* act.

Why?

Because when you do that, you've got a completely different anchor than you did before. When Jesus is your best friend, you

know you're accepted completely by the only One who matters —
God. You know that while Jesus wants you to do the best with what
gifts you have, Jesus is also not judging you on any of those achieve-
ments or identities your parents, your friends, your culture are telling
you that you must have in order to be important and valued.

In short — with Jesus: no holding back. With Jesus, you're free.

And as a disciple of Jesus, you take that sense of freedom out
into the world, into the way you live your life, and there's no reason to lie anymore.

In fact, the whole idea of cheating instead of really learning, of
lying, of ripping off other people's stuff, of pretending to be what
you're not, becomes less and less an option. It just doesn't occur to
you.

Because you know what Jesus said: *". . . the truth will make you
free"* (John 8:32).

Let's get practical for a minute and work through some issues.
Again, we don't have the space to go through individual cases, but

The first place to work on honesty is with God. In your
prayer, in your inner life with God, don't hold anything back.
Be who you are. Argue, praise, thank, be sad and confused.
God wants to hear all of it.

The second place is . . . yourself. How honest are you about
yourself *with* yourself, anyway? How honest are you about:

- Your weaknesses?
- Your strengths?
- Your pain, regret, and fears?

How honest are you about the power and influence other
people and the culture have over you? You can't grow as a
person unless you admit to the power of the messages you're
resisting.

if you can simply understand what the attitude of a friend of Jesus should be to questions of honesty . . . that's a start.

It's not easy to be honest with parents, and it's not always your fault. One of the complaints I regularly heard from my students was:

"If I were honest with my parents about what I was doing, they'd never let me go out and I'd never be able to do anything fun."

I really don't know how to answer that except to say . . . reverse roles. Just for a minute.

Imagine that you're the parent and your kid is lying to you about what he's doing Friday night and where he's going, and he's doing what you're doing right now.

Would you be happy about that?

Just think about it.

> **Dost thou hate to be deceived? Do not deceive another.**
>
> — St. John Chrysostom, *Homilies*

Another complaint I regularly heard from my students was:

"I want to be honest with my parents, but if they knew what I was really thinking and feeling, they would be so mad and disappointed in me."

Again, reverse roles. If you were a parent, and your daughter was going through some really tough times . . . would you want them to hide it or be honest?

It's hard, because some parents *will* overreact, and not all parents can handle every truth about their kids well. If there's something really important that you're lying about, but you're honestly afraid of your parents' reaction, and you have good reason to be, based on past experience . . . tell another adult. Please. And then go from there.

I also heard this one from my students:

"My parents lie to *me*. My parents cheat on their taxes.
They brag about it. I guess I can, too."

No. Parents are to be respected — it's a commandment, you
know — but parents are people. Some parents are saints, others are
not. Your ultimate role model is Jesus. You're His disciple, not your
parents'. If they're doing wrong — they're doing wrong. That's not
an excuse for you to do wrong.

By the way — here's one thing that being honest does not mean.

It doesn't mean saying something true but hurtful to someone
just to hurt them, and then walk away, shrugging and saying, "Well,
I'm supposed to be honest, aren't I?"

Even virtues can be turned into weapons. Don't.

Prudence is a virtue, too.

> You are asked to get rid of your sins, not to
> show that others have committed the like.
> — St. John Chrysostom,
> in *1 Cor Homilies XIV*

So, it really all comes down to this:

Our reasons for dishonesty vary, but they all seem to come
down to this in the end: the desire for some kind of freedom — usu-
ally a freedom from suffering.

Problem is, dishonesty slams us in prison. A prison of self-decep-
tion, in which we don't know who we are anymore, in which we're
not truthful with God or anyone else. And amazingly enough . . . we
still suffer.

They don't call it "web of lies" for nothing.

Thomas said to him, "Lord, we do not know where you are going; how can we know the way?" Jesus said to him, "I am the way, and the truth, and the life; no one comes to the Father, but by me."

— John 14:5-6

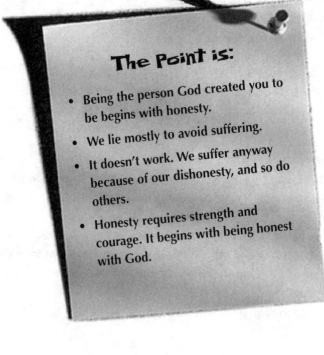

The Point is:

- Being the person God created you to be begins with honesty.

- We lie mostly to avoid suffering.

- It doesn't work. We suffer anyway because of our dishonesty, and so do others.

- Honesty requires strength and courage. It begins with being honest with God.

CHAPTER 5

I've Got All the Time in the World... Don't I?

LOTS OF CHOICES out there. Hard to choose.

It's a problem for little kids. Maybe that little kid was you once upon a time. A time when simple questions such as "What flavor ice cream do you want?" can bring an entire line of people to a total standstill while they wait, wait, wait. . .

Until finally a mom snaps, "I'm going to count to ten — no five — and you have to decide by then."

Maybe you still feel like that little child in front of the ice cream counter sometimes.

Do I *really* have to decide my college major? Now?

The clock is ticking, though. You don't have forever. You *have* to decide sometime.

Yes, the clock is really ticking, even if it's digital and really just buzzes. Work with me. Because it's ticking.

Which clock?

How about the one that started running when you were conceived and that's going to stop . . .

. . . someday?

I DON'T MEAN TO depress you, and I really hope you're *not* depressed. Because, of course, the clock of your life doesn't actually stop ticking the moment you die. You're a human being, so that means you have an immortal soul. Which means you were created by God to live forever, and created in love by that same God because He wants you to live forever with *Him*.

So in a sense, the clock doesn't stop ticking.

Yay!

But in another sense, it does.

Boo!

And in what sense would that be?

In the sense that, quite simply, the time we have on earth to make our choice on whether we are going to live that eternal life with God or not is limited.

It's more than five seconds your mom gave you to pick a flavor, true. And right now it may seem like plenty of time. But it's not.

If someone close to you has died — especially someone young — you know this painfully well. The reality that life on earth is

rather shockingly short and we don't know when our last breath will come probably hit you hard when you first realized it, but the impact of that realization has faded as you've gotten swept up in the busy-ness of life.

But as morbid as it sounds, it's important to keep that recognition of the ticking clock in our consciousness, front and center. One of the most powerful statements of the Christian awareness of this, and the importance it should play in our lives, comes down to two simple Latin words:

Memento Mori —

which means:

Remember, You Will Die.

Not exactly what the voices around us sing, is it? No, their song is more like: "Spend a lot of money on our stuff and fantasize that you'll live forever!" Or something like that.

Wow. How morbid. You know, I am really sorry about that, but it's just a fact. Your time on earth is limited, and so one of the deepest, persistent moral questions you and I face, every day, is this one:

How am I using my time?

Think about it. If someone gives you a gift — oh, let's say an amazing new cell phone or mp3 player, and you say, "Er, thanks," and then toss it in the closet (not that you would do that, I'm thinking) right in front of them . . . wow. What an insult. What a mean thing to do. "Mean" as in "immoral." Right?

Not too much different here. Get your head out of the worldly space and back into the God Space we're trying to think in now, the space where the disciples walk with Jesus on the journey.

Your life is a gift. Your time is a gift.

How you use that gift of time is a — moral choice. It really is.

And like all the rest of our moral choices, our habits, our virtues, our small choices train us, in a way, for how we make the big choices.

So ... if we're in the habit of thinking about the time we have *today* in the right way, in a way that's consistent with being a disciple of Jesus, then we'll eventually build the habit of thinking of that bigger chunk of time called *our whole lives* in that God-soaked context.

So. What did you do last night?

> **Man is like a breath; his days are like a passing shadow.**
>
> — Psalm 144:4

Obviously, the opposite of using time well is wasting it. And wasting time is, whether we want to admit it or not, not what we're put on earth to do. To put it simply:

There's something sinful about wasting time.

But wait ... wait ... wait.

What does it mean to "waste" time?

In our busy, busy culture in which even teens have incredibly complicated schedules, "wasting" time seems to mean, "having a block of time that's not booked."

That's not it at all, because, believe it or not, busy, busy time can be wasted time, too.

And, to make it even more complicated, an hour spent sitting outside doing "nothing" can actually be the opposite of wasted time. That hour just might be the best and most moral use of time you've had today.

It's so confusing!

Look. There are some activities that really, in and of themselves, are wasted. I'm going out on a limb here and suggesting that ten hours spent in front of a television watching mindless 1980s sitcoms *might* fall into that category. Getting hooked into playing a video game until you beat the thing, no matter how many days it's going to take, might, too. Just maybe.

When you're trying to figure out if you're using your time well —
that is, morally — the way that Jesus' friends will use the gift of time
— there are a few questions that you can ask to help you figure it out.
You don't have to answer "yes" to all of them. One will do.

- Is what I'm doing during this time helping me grow as a person?
- Is this time spent fulfilling a responsibility?
- Is this time spent helping someone?
- Is this time spent honoring the one who gave me these minutes?

In short . . . am I growing at all in holiness with the way I'm
spending this time?

DO NOT STOP READING!

I know you want to, because that all probably sounds very seventeenth-century, let's-all-sit-in-the-parlor and be-very-painfully-quiet to
you. Very, Very, Responsible and Serious.

Well, work with me on this one, because the truth is, that not-having-fun part is simply not the Catholic way of doing things.

God didn't put Adam and Eve on a bench in the middle of a
room, after all. He put them in a garden: as in *life, beauty, fertility,
joyfulness, diversity, and peace.*

God is truth. He's life and joy and beauty. Being holy, living as
God's image, being a disciple of Jesus is about all of that. Pursuing
beauty and enjoyment and happy times is not — repeat *not* —
wasting time.

After all, remember how Jesus was perceived. This is what He
said about His own reputation among the self-proclaimed righteous:

> *"The Son of Man has come eating and drinking; and you
> say, 'Behold, a glutton and a drunkard, a friend of tax-collectors and sinners!' "* (LUKE 7:34)

Reading between the lines, what you see is that Jesus was accused of, well . . . partying too much. With the wrong kind of people.

Which is, you might be interested to know, the Catholic way, all the way.

The Catholic way — forged through centuries of life in cities and villages all over the globe, shaped by our Jewish heritage and the rhythms of life, is about feasts and celebrations. It's about gorgeous art, heroic, gripping stories, theater and music, games, big, rollicking families and adventure.

There have been Christians who frowned on all of that, who did, indeed, make their children sit indoors on Sundays in stiff clothes on hard benches, yearning for the outdoors. Those people were called Puritans, and when they came to America, it was very important to them to ban Christmas, and not just because Christmas means "Christ's Mass," and that was all way-too-Catholic for them. No — they were reacting against the Catholic way of celebration and feast.

> On this mountain the LORD of hosts will make for all peoples a feast of fat things, a feast of choice wines — of fat things full of marrow, of choice wines well refined.
>
> — Isaiah 25:6

So, using your time in a way that's faithful to Jesus isn't just determined by the activity itself. As Jesus tells us again and again — our inner disposition, our intention is important. Let's see how this works:

- Going to a party for the purpose of getting drunk or high: a waste. Even worse — damaging. Hence: sinful.
- Going to a party, staying straight, enjoying time with friends: not a waste.

- Spending hours on the computer mindlessly chatting: a waste.

- Spending less-than-hours on the computer chatting with a friend who needs advice or just needs to vent and following it up with face time, you know, between two human beings in the same room: not a waste.

- Spending a year engaged in some activity that you don't care about, don't enjoy, and wouldn't be doing unless everyone was telling you that you *had* to have it on your résumé or the *best* colleges won't take you: a waste.

- Spending a year fascinated by an activity that you're passionate about and that touches your creative, intellectual, athletic, or charitable side: not a waste

- Spending the afternoon at the mall wishing you could buy all kinds of stuff, or spending a lot of money on things you don't need: a waste

- Spending the afternoon at the mall, window-shopping, buying a few things, enjoying time with friends: not a waste.

You probably get the idea. But be careful, too. Because there really aren't hard and fast rules that you can apply across the board. Some points to remember:

- Even if we're guilty of wasting time, God is present in those moments. God's there. He's working in your life, somehow. Are you listening?

- Our legitimate passions can, if we're not careful, become harmful. They can become ways that we escape from connecting with people, or from responsibility. The trick is to use the time we spend on our passions to really develop into the whole, healthy people God wants us to be, and to connect and serve others through our interests. To figure out how this works, observe the adults around you. How often do their

work and other kinds of passions and interests function to take them away from family, instead of serving family?

One big warning:

You can't judge the value of how you're spending your time by your personal desires or emotions, either.

(In fact, you can't judge the morality of *any* act by desires and emotions. Learn that now, save time later.)

Most people don't want to take most of the subjects they take in school. They might even call them a "waste." Truthfully, some of it might be — any teacher will admit there's way too much wasted time in a school day.

But the fact is — there you are. If you want to meet the goal — that diploma — this is what you've got to do.

> "Then run, faithful souls, happy and tireless, keep up with your beloved who marches with giant strides from one end of heaven to the other. Nothing is hidden from his eyes. . .. Wherever you go he has gone before. Only follow him and you will find him everywhere."
> — Jean-Pierre de Causaade,
> *The Sacrament of the Present Moment*, 65

Same with jobs. After the initial thrill of being in the workforce and getting those first few paychecks wears off, popping fries into the grease vat seems like less and less of a great way to spend time.

Oh well. It's called *work*. And spending our time working is the way we're obligated to spend time to earn our keep in the world. People eat French fries, which means someone's got to cook them. Might as well be you!

So don't turn this around and make it all about whether or not you feel fulfilled or not, or whether or not you're really, really thrilled to be in geometry class.

GROWING TO BE the person God created us to be, being a disciple of Jesus means using the time we're given to grow in holiness. We keep coming back to the brain shift a disciple of Jesus has to be willing to undergo, and this is a big part of it.

We can grow in holiness doing all kinds of things:

- Enjoying time with friends
- Sharing meals
- Volunteering
- Enjoying the arts
- Creating
- Competing
- Studying
- Working
- Staring into space, thinking.
- Praying
- Serving others in small ways
- Fulfilling our duties and responsibilities

I'm thinking you get the idea.

Using the gift of time morally isn't always easy, because being a disciple of Jesus isn't easy. We have to sacrifice, and even suffer — a little or a lot. We don't always have fun.

MAYBE THIS WHOLE discussion struck you as weird at the beginning of this chapter. How can how I spend Saturday afternoon be a "moral choice?" I hope it makes more sense now:

- We can't split our lives into parts: the part that's about God and the part that's about us. If we do, we're guilty of living a Sunday-only kind of faith, and that's just not faith.
- Your Christian faith is about being a disciple of Jesus: following Him and walking with Him because you love Him. All the time.
- Your Christian faith is about shaping your life after Jesus', your best friend — thinking like Him, seeing with His eyes, loving like He does.
- All of this starts with time. It happens in time.
- Growing in holiness doesn't mean doing it tomorrow, or during the 23 hours and 45 minutes a day you're not praying. It means . . . *now.*
- It means living this gift of time in this gift of creation with a heart that's so, so grateful that we can't imagine *not* using our time to grow in holiness.

Because, you know, you are going to be asked someday . . . "I gave you a gift. And . . . what did you do with it?"

> "Everyone to whom much is given, of him will much be required; and of him to whom men commit much they will demand the more."
> — Luke 12:48

The Point is:

- Time is a precious gift from God. It's a sin to waste it.

- Using time well and with gratitude to God means using what He's given us to grow as people, grow in love of others, create and serve others. That can be hard, and it can be fun, too.

CHAPTER 6

Love Who? Everyone? Really?

IT WOULD BE REALLY pretty easy to be virtuous, be that disciple of Jesus, if it weren't for one big problem.

Those other people. Yeah. *Them.*

I MEAN, THERE YOU ARE, your head and heart in exactly the right place, ready to be nice, to be super-kind, to say nothing but nice things . . . and you go downstairs for breakfast and your mom is *in a mood.*

Try again. You make it to school, ready again to be that disciple, to follow Jesus, no illusions that it's going to be easy . . . and you turn the corner and there is *that* guy. That guy who you just can't stand for a million reasons, including the fact that he cheated on your best friend and he stole your biology folder and copied your homework.

Can we try this one more time?

Can I do this love thing — this *commandment* — with someone who's not so hard to love, and when I'm in a better mood?

> "Love means loving the unlovable — or it is no virtue at all."
> — G.K. Chesterton, *Heretics*

What an immense pain. And so, so frustrating, isn't it? To really be committed to being good and kind, only to be tripped up every time by the fact that the people you're trying to be nice to just won't cooperate.

Makes you just want to give up, doesn't it?

> "For if you love those who love you, what reward have you? Do not even the tax collectors do the same? And if you salute only your brethren, what more are you doing than others? Do not even the Gentiles do the same? You, therefore, must be perfect, as your heavenly Father is perfect."
>
> — Matthew 5:46-48

Oh.

Well, maybe not. Perfect? But . . . *how*?

Living as a disciple of Jesus involves a lot of relationships. With God, ourselves, and others.

Yes, those others. We've talked a bit about the fundamentals of a virtuous life — the virtues themselves, being honest, not throwing the gift of time away. But there's one more general point we need to cover before we get to those specifics about moral choices.

And that is . . . what should our general attitude toward others be? How should you see them? What should you expect them to be?

Because, you see, when you've got this covered, the specifics of morality just make a lot more sense.

To figure out what exactly this involves, we don't have to look far. After all, the goal here is to be a faithful, joyful disciple of Jesus. Disciple means "student." So when we're learning how to view others, we're going to have to sit down and be students of Jesus.

How did Jesus treat others?

⤵ With honesty.

We've covered honesty before, but let's look at it from a different angle. Jesus was honest about who He was, and honest about other people as well. He saw their sinfulness, and named it. He saw their essential goodness and the passionate love God had for them, and He lived it, treating every person with the dignity and respect they deserve.

> But when they heard it, they went away, one by one, beginning with the eldest, and Jesus was left alone with the woman standing before him. Jesus looked up and said to her, "Woman, where are they? Has no one condemned you?" She said, "No one, Lord." And Jesus said, "Neither do I condemn you; go, and do not sin again."
>
> — John 8:9-11

What does that mean for us? It doesn't mean randomly naming people's weaknesses and mistakes. (*Prudence* — remember prudence.) It doesn't mean self-righteousness. After all, Jesus is something we're not. God, that is.

No, we're talking attitudes here. Attitudes that will eventually work their way into actions, but that have to be planted within us to take root and grow.

So . . . like Jesus, we're honest to ourselves about other people's limitations, potential, and identity. We don't expect other people to be gods. We don't hold them up to impossible standards of perfection. We're honest about their capacity to hurt us. We're honest about their surprising capacity to love. We're honest, most importantly, about God's love for them. Each one. Even the ones who bug us the most. *Especially* them.

With humility.

Jesus, Lord of Creation, Son of God, walked among us, loving us, serving us. He is humility.

> So if there is any encouragement in Christ, any incentive of love, any participation in the Spirit, any affection and sympathy, complete my joy by being of the same mind, having the same love, being in full accord and of one mind. Do nothing from selfishness or conceit, but in humility count others better than yourselves.
>
> — Philippians 2:1-3

For us, being all human, and not a bit God, humility means something very simple: Understanding that God loves everyone — even our worst enemies — as much as He loves us. We're all sinners, we all have the same capacity for holiness. Our particular gifts

don't make us more worthy or better than anyone else. Other people's talents don't make them better than us, either. We don't judge other people's sins — we recognize them and try to correct them, but most of all, we love.

↳ With forgiveness.

We barely have to say anything about this. We just have to look, again, at that crucifix, and listen to Jesus.

If Jesus, from that cross, can forgive . . . why can't I?

Now, this doesn't mean being a doormat and letting people hurt and abuse us. People have to be held accountable — so if someone harms you, you must tell someone in authority. It's not loving to let someone go on thinking that they can harm others without consequences.

But when it comes to the personal dynamic between you and someone who's hurt you, there's one question you might ask yourself as you struggle with the decision whether or not to let go of your anger and pray for the person who's hurt you instead.

"Why not?"

That is . . . why not forgive?

And Jesus said, "Father, forgive them; for they know not what they do."
— Luke 23:34

↳ With compassion.

Do you know what "compassion" means?

Well, "passion" means strong, deep feelings or experiences, with a particular sub-definition meaning "suffering."

"Com" is a Latin prefix that means "with."

So "compassion" means . . . to suffer with.

When you have compassion for another person, you suffer with that person. You empathize. You join yourself to them in their pain.

Jesus was . . . compassionate.

He was compassionate in the small moments, as He answered the plea of the suffering.

He was also compassionate in that most important moment in history, when God reached down and joined himself to every suffering person on earth, suffering himself until the point of death.

That . . . is compassion.

Do you remember who we are?

Disciples . . . of Jesus? Students?

So when we encounter others, we meet them with an attitude. No, not *that* attitude. An attitude of honesty, humility, forgiveness, and compassion.

People are difficult. People are hateful. People will, indeed, hurt you and laugh about it later.

No one knows that better than Jesus.

But still . . . compassion.

Not excuses. Not letting people off the hook or releasing them from responsibility or consequences. That's not loving, either. But . . compassion.

> As he drew near to Jericho, a blind man was sitting by the roadside begging; and hearing a multitude going by, he inquired what this meant. They told him, "Jesus of Nazareth is passing by." And he cried, "Jesus, Son of David, have mercy on me!" And those who were in front rebuked him, telling him to be silent; but he cried out all the more, "Son of David, have mercy on me!" And Jesus stopped, and commanded him to be brought to

him; and when he came near, he asked him,
"What do you want me to do for you?" He
said, "Lord, let me receive my sight." And
Jesus said to him, "Receive your sight; your
faith has made you well."

— Luke 18:35-42

???

ONE OF THE HARDEST THINGS about being a disciple of Jesus today is that we're surrounded by so many illusions, so many false messages about what we should expect out of life.

Unfortunately, some of those illusions get filtered to us through churchy kinds of channels, not just the world's.

So, for example, we develop this idea that if we just try to be a "good person," sunshine will fill our days, flowers will spring up in our footsteps, and everyone we meet will be so moved by our efforts that they will respond with a smile and a hug, and the world will be at peace.

And full of lots of hugs.

Like I said . . . an illusion.

An illusion that you absolutely will not find in the Christian story, as it's really told in the Bible and in the spiritual tradition of the Church.

To get this, just remember the central symbol of your Christian faith, what disciples always recognize as the sign of who they are. What is it?

Flowers?

Bunnies?

A sunshiney meadow?

No.

It's a cross.

Hanging on that cross is a man who was, I think you'll agree, the best person who ever lived. Who treated all He met with love and compassion — the love and compassion of God, because that's who He is. Completely innocent in every way.

So sure, look at that cross, and consider how people responded to that compassion and love.

They nailed Him to a cross. They killed Him.

And keep considering . . . even then . . . how did He respond?

HERE'S THE THING you just have to get as you start walking this journey as a disciple of Jesus, and that everyone further along the journey has to remind themselves of every day:

We are made to be with God. We're made in His image, which means we were made to love, and we won't find real, deep lasting joy until we are loving as God loves, embodied in the love of Jesus on the cross. The Resurrection follows — after the Cross.

You can't start walking if you expect that the world is going to reward you for loving, forgiving, sacrificing, and caring in that truly radical way of Jesus.

You can't be in it for the praise or the acceptance and the glory *here on earth.*

And every time you forget that . . . look up at that crucifix.

Boy, we just keep heaping on the harsh, don't we?

It's not harsh. It's just real. And I think you probably know it, too.

After all, think about the reasons you give yourself not to be open about following Jesus . . . what are a lot of those reasons about?

How other people are going to react, maybe?

That you'll be mocked, rejected and just generally treated differently?

So, yeah, you know it. You know what a disciple of Jesus can expect.

There is no living in love without suffering.
— Thomas à Kempis,
Imitation of Christ, 3.5

If you want to know how true that is . . . ask your parents. Ask them about love and suffering and all that. They might be able to tell you something.

But . . . you might be saying . . . Jesus was God . . . how am I supposed to do this? I'm not exactly God. How in the world is it possible?

Okay, then. This is the part where we turn back to those virtues — the theological virtues, remember? The ones that we develop with the grace of God? Paul knew all about them, and he reminds us of the basic attitude that motivates the disciples of Jesus:

> *"So faith, hope, love abide, these three; but the greatest of these is love."* (1 CORINTHIANS 13:13)

Looking at others as Jesus does is not something that we can have a lesson plan for. There are no workshops or strategies or sure-fire steps that will get us there.

We can only develop this attitude if we are committed to seeing with the eyes of Christ . . . letting Christ live in us and love through us:

> *I have been crucified with Christ; it is no longer I who live, but Christ who lives in me. . . .* (GALATIANS 2:20)

So . . . how do you do that? How do you grow in that friendship, share that mind of Christ, let Christ live and love in and through you?

Simple:

⤶ Love Jesus as your best friend. Be open to whatever He tells you, as Mary said to the folks who ran out of wine at Cana. Just do it.

⤶ Read the Scriptures. Know Jesus.

⤶ Pray. Not just random thoughts in your head, but the ancient prayers that disciples have always prayed. The Rosary. The Psalms. Morning and Evening Prayer. Get a Catholic prayer book and pray.

⤶ Celebrate the Sacrament of Reconciliation regularly — once a month, if you can. Let Jesus touch you with His forgiveness and healing, and let that live in you.

⤶ Most importantly, most amazingly . . . receive Jesus so that He really does live within you, so that He really does nourish you and strengthen you for this hard, hard road that will, He promises, end in joy. It's called Eucharist. It's called the Mass.

And when you do go to Mass, try something new: pray. Join together with all of the other Catholics through history, around the world, who go into their churches, think about their own lives and their own walk with Jesus, and offer it up. They join their own sacrifices — the difficulties of really loving, the rejection, the pain, the suffering . . . and join it with Jesus' suffering on the cross, His self-sacrifice of His own Body and Blood.

And then, right there, you're joined with Him.

$$? \quad ? \quad ?$$

THIS JOURNEY takes a lifetime. We go forward and backward, we get discouraged.

But remember. . .

The virtuous life isn't just about us and God. It's about us, God, and every other person on earth and all of creation. It's a cosmic

journey we're on, a journey with *other people* whom we're called to *love* because God loves them.

Even when it hurts.

Especially when it hurts.

> The poor you may have right in your own family. We get many young people coming to our place, to Calcutta, to share the joy of loving, and it's beautiful to see how devotedly they serve the poorest of the poor, with so much love, with so much care. And many families have got to see in their own family the suffering, the pain and the loneliness. . . You have many poor people here. Find them, love them, put your love for them in living action, for in loving them, you are loving God Himself.
>
> — Mother Teresa,
> Harvard University, June 1982

The Point is:

- Love is the greatest commandment, the commandment Jesus gave us.

- Love is difficult.

- Love means seeing others through the eyes of Christ. We can only do this when we're connected to Christ and let Him love through us.

- In love, we treat others with honesty, humility, forgiveness, and compassion.

CHAPTER 7

It's My Body. All Mine.

WE SKIPPED SOMETHING.

Way back there in those early chapters, when we were figuring out who you are and what you're about, we left something out.

Your body, maybe?

> . . . then the LORD God formed man of dust from the ground, and breathed into his nostrils the breath of life; and man became a living soul.
>
> — Genesis 2:7

As God breathes into the man whose body He's formed, so He shapes every one of us, and that means *you*.

We are creatures made of body and soul. What we do with that body matters. What we do with our bodies is a moral issue: that is, something that has the power to bring us closer to God . . . or further away.

And that means *you*. And *your body*.

???

SO YES, there are those moments. Moments that we have to decide, very concretely, what to do with our hands, our lips, how physically intimate to get with someone else, in the midst of all of the fever, emotion, desire, and physical pressure. Somehow, in all of that, we have to be able to remember that God has just as much to do with what we're doing right now as He has to do with our decisions whether or not to be honest, to speak kindly, to be responsible.

It matters.

We spend a lot of time trying to convince ourselves that it doesn't, though. We think that we can separate it all out and that Jesus doesn't really care about what's going on in the back seat or at parties or with us in front of the computer.

Sorry . . . He does.

Sometimes you'll hear people say, "Well, Jesus didn't talk much about sex, you know. He talked a whole lot more about the *poor*. So why are Christians so obsessed with sex?" Well . . .

- Look around. Watch some TV. Listen to some music. It's *Christians* who are obsessed with *sex*? Really?

- It's always interesting to ask folks who are into comparing what Jesus explicitly said about sex and about the poor . . . how much of *their* time and resources they're devoting to what Jesus talked most about. The answer might surprise you. Or not.

- There's a reason Jesus didn't go around laying down rules and being specific about sexual morality: Jesus was preaching to His fellow Jews. He preached about new things, about the Good News that was . . . new. If He didn't mention sexual morality, that was because the Jewish teaching on sexual morality didn't need anything "new" brought into it.

In other words, Genesis 1 and 2 still apply.

If I learned anything about young people in the years I've spent teaching and raising them, it's that you guys have superb, precise Hypocrisy Detectors. It's one of your favorite pastimes — to call out older people on their hypocrisy. And that's a good thing. We need it.

But here's something else to think about.

If you're walking around bearing that name of Christian, but *you* decide that Jesus has nothing to do with what you do with your body and your sexuality . . . there's a name for that.

You get one guess what it is.

???

NOW, THERE ARE ALL kinds of specific strategies on how to deal with these issues and lots to say about the specifics. We'll do a lot of specifics in the next chapter. But first we have to deal with the basics that are going to apply to *any* situation *anywhere.*

Quite simply: What is the attitude of a disciple of Jesus toward his or her own body?

Well, since we're "disciples" — students, that means we have a teacher. And we know who that is.

Jesus had a body. He was the Word made Flesh, remember?

How did Jesus use His body?

Obviously, this is not the space for specifics. First of all, Jesus wasn't married, and most of you will probably end up married, so those particulars don't apply. There are, simply, too many various particulars and situations to list, anyway.

You're a disciple of Jesus, so in answering that question, you look to Jesus, a man like us in all things but sin. A human being with friends and family, who shared meals, who drank, who walked and worked, touched and was touched.

Think about all you know about Jesus.

What was His body for? How did He live in and through that body?

Well, let's see. Just let your mind wander through the Gospels. What do you see, what do you remember?

Jesus used His hands . . . to heal and comfort.

His voice . . . to share the Good News of God's love and mercy.

His feet . . . to walk the earth, right to the places where people needed Him.

Finally, Jesus gave . . . His whole self to the Father for us, suffering in body, dying out of passionate, committed love. Holding nothing back, for us.

There's your starting point — to immerse yourself in that, to be committed to using the gift of your body in the same way Jesus did:

> *Now as they were eating, Jesus took bread, and blessed, and broke it, and gave it to the disciples and said, "Take, eat; this is my body." And he took a chalice, and when he*

*had given thanks he gave it to them, saying, 'Drink of it,
all of you; for this is my blood of the covenant, which is
poured out for many for the forgiveness of sins.* (MATTHEW
26:26-28)

And do you know what? When it's Saturday night, and it's you
and that other person and you're feeling passionate . . .

. . . none of that — *none of it* — stops being true.

Not even for a minute.

DO YOU BELIEVE THAT?

Really? Do you?

The truly difficult part about all of this sexuality business is that
even if we have the best of intentions, the combination of where our
bodies and emotions are at, physically and very naturally, along
with a really permissive culture, has a certain amount of power over
us.

There's pleasure in knowing others think you're hot.

There's pleasure in *feeling* hot.

There's pleasure in physical intimacy.

After all, if all of that (and more) was *unpleasant* . . . we wouldn't
be here talking, would we?

It's not *temptation* unless it's pleasurable or satisfying in some
way.

THAT'S WHY IT IS SO, so important to really not just know what your
values are, but commit to them and live them out in small ways.

Because here's the thing, and it's really something that no one is
willing to be honest about with you:

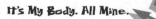

It's My Body. All Mine. **79**

When you're hot and heavy — with others or alone, frankly — there comes a point, a tipping point, at which even the most well-intentioned person . . . *just doesn't care.*

It's physical. It's chemical. It's what your body is leading you to because, in case you didn't catch this part of the biology lesson, all of those body parts are there and work the way they do when they do for a reason: to make a baby.

It's why we get aroused and excited, it's why we feel propelled and *compelled* to just *keep going* and why it's so hard to stop.

Our bodies don't *want* us to stop.

Stupid bodies.

Or maybe — smart bodies. Maybe the fact that our bodies do this is a huge clue as to what the purpose of all of this is and why we shouldn't be messing around unless we're ready and willing to go ahead and let those bodies go the whole way and make those amazing babies — brand new little people, little beloved children of God — in a family that will care and love them the way God cares and loves us: with unswerving commitment, rock-like stability and self-sacrifice.

(They call it marriage, by the way.)

???

That's all general, but I hope you see how powerful and true it really is. You're here on earth for a reason: to love, to know, and to serve God. The way you do this is specific to you and your talents. But in the end, that's what it comes down to, and when you're facing eternity, that's what will be asked of you:

- How did you use these gifts?
- How did you treat your body?
- How did you treat the bodies of others?

Was it all about you and your few seconds of pleasure, or was it about love — real love — that brings joy that lasts a *lot* longer than a few seconds?

Chastity

There's a name for the attitude, stance and practice we're talking about in this chapter. It's called "chastity."

We often think of chastity as just saying no to premarital sex. That's not the correct definition — because even married people are called to be chaste. All human beings are called to live in the world chastely.

So what does it mean?

Everything we've been talking about. Understanding what your body is for and living that way. Understanding what sexuality is all about and living it:

> "Chastity is really a way to look at all your relationships so that they no longer become mere exchanges of commodities. It's a plan for your whole life, for your happiness, and for eventually going to heaven. I look at chastity as a way to practice what it's like to be in heaven."
>
> — DAWN EDEN, AUTHOR OF *THE THRILL OF THE CHASTE*,
> INTERVIEW IN *THE LONG ISLAND CATHOLIC*,
> MARCH 7, 2007

(So . . . how can married people be unchaste? Well, married people can be tempted to use each other as objects, to use sex as a weapon in a relationship, to close off their sexuality to the possibility of making babies — that's all *definitely* unchaste.)

So this reality, which we just can't deny. It's also really, really serious. Consider the misery of people you know who've been exploited sexually, who have profound regrets about things they've done that they can't undo . . . serious, life-changing stuff here.

So how can we live this out? Everything — the culture, our own hormones and desires — seems against us. What can we do? Start here:

- Commit yourself to live your whole life, body and soul, as a disciple of Jesus. In prayer, however you can, maybe even in front of Jesus' Real Presence of *His* Body and Blood, soul and divinity — commit. Promise. And pray for help.

- Bring all of your temptations to Jesus in prayer. *All* of them.

- Go to confession. *Confess.* Let Jesus' mercy strengthen you. You can always, always, always start over. Always. Did you hear that? What did I say? *Always.*

- Receive Jesus in the Eucharist often. Let His love fill you. Join your whole self to Him. Pray: *Live in me. Love others through me.*

And maybe, just maybe . . . think about being a little bit radical here.

Be honest about the power of this culture. Be honest about the hothouse that your peer group is. And maybe . . . walk apart. Just a little. Not in a snobbish, arrogant way. But in this way:

- Dress modestly, which simply means dress in a way that doesn't scream, "Look at my breasts! Look at my rear end! Look . . . everywhere!" (Guys and girls both.)

- Have some reserve with people of the opposite sex. Don't talk about sexual matters with them.

- Think about the music you listen to and the images you let into your brain. Then rethink it.

Finally, consider this. Now this might be the point that makes you shut the book and just go elsewhere, but too bad. I really think it's worth thinking about:

↳ Re-think the whole concept of dating.

I'm not going to dictate *how* you should rethink it or what you should conclude, but think about it, anyway. Think about an alternative world in which you're not concerned about who's going out with who or if someone likes you or not, or worried about how far to go on a date or how someone talks to you after you go out . . . or any of that.

It is possible for teenagers to find love and to love. Some of you might even be the child or grandchild of men and women who did, indeed, find lasting love in their teens. It happens.

But it used to happen more frequently when the culture was a little different. When the expectation — even if it wasn't lived out perfectly all the time — was that sexual activity wasn't just recreational and came with responsibility and the majority of folks who were in high school were getting ready, not to go off to college for even more school, but to plunge right into adult life. It was a different world that your grandparents lived in. Not our world, a world in which sex means something different — and you're under incredible pressure to internalize that casual, recreational definition of sex into the way you live your life.

But even if it's possible, it's rare. And sometimes the most powerful step we can take in our lives is just to admit — remember how important *honesty* is in trying to live a virtuous life — to admit that:

↳ We are weak.
↳ Our culture and our desires are very strong.
↳ We're not superheroes. We need help.
↳ We sometimes need to take radical steps to protect ourselves. To make it *easier* to live as a disciple . . . to find happiness.

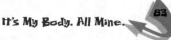

Yeah, so imagine it. Imagine what it would be like to be free from all of those obsessions and concerns, and to trust that all that really matters in life is God's love, not some seventeen-year-old guy or girl's judgment of your appearance or sexual experience, or their expectations of what you can do for *them*.

And you wonder why they call it . . . *Good News*.

> We should love others truly, for their own sakes rather than our own.
> — St. Thomas Aquinas,
> *Summa Theologica*, 2-2, 184, 1

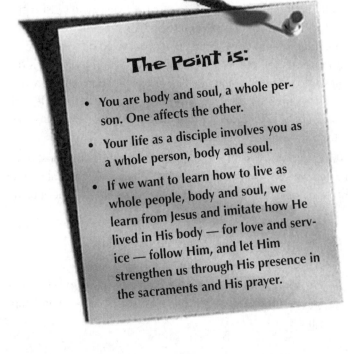

The Point is:

- You are body and soul, a whole person. One affects the other.

- Your life as a disciple involves you as a whole person, body and soul.

- If we want to learn how to live as whole people, body and soul, we learn from Jesus and imitate how He lived in His body — for love and service — follow Him, and let Him strengthen us through His presence in the sacraments and His prayer.

CHAPTER 8

How Far Can I Go?

THAT LAST CHAPTER might have left you in a kind of confused, irony-soaked mess. I hope not, but it's possible. Let's regroup for just a moment before we go on:

- God made us. God built the keys to our lasting happiness into our souls and bodies. We need to listen and learn.
- Jesus teaches us, very concretely, what our bodies are for: to love and serve God and others.
- If Jesus is our teacher, He's our teacher about *everything* all the time.
- It's difficult, but not impossible to live this way. Jesus strengthens us in prayer, healthy friendships, and the sacraments.
- To live this way — chastely — is a radical choice in today's culture.
- To live this way is incredibly freeing.

Now, let's get specific.

Speaking the Language of Our Bodies

JEWISH AND CHRISTIAN tradition, reflective of God's revelation, has always taught the truth about sexuality and its proper place in life. When you read the Scriptures and listen to the traditions of Christianity, you hear a consistent message from Genesis 1 on.

In recent years, a slightly new way of thinking about this truth has emerged and become very popular. It's called the "Theology of the Body."

We can thank Pope John Paul II for the Theology of the Body. Besides being a priest and bishop, Pope John Paul was a great philosopher and theologian as well. As a philosopher, he was very interested in what it means to be a human person. He was also interested in language — which makes sense, since language is one of the things that really distinguishes human beings from the rest of the animal world.

Beginning in 1981, Pope John Paul gave a series of talks during his "General Audiences" — the public gatherings that take place every Wednesday with the Pope, mostly in St. Peter's Square, unless the weather is bad (then they move inside to a hall) or the Pope is on vacation.

In this particular set of 129 talks, which have been collected into a book, the Pope talked about sexuality — for more than two years! — and the relationships between men and women, what our bodies are for, and, most importantly, how all of this — every bit of it — is a reflection of God's love for us.

In short, the Theology of the Body comes down to this:

↳ Our bodies communicate truths about who we are and why God made us.

↳ The fundamental truth we see is that we are created to love. Everything else flows from this.

↳ Love is not lust or just an emotion. Love is defined by God's identity as a Trinity of Love, and God's love for us: it is free, it is faithful, it is total and it is sacrificial.

↳ God's love is fruitful and creative and builds bonds of community.

↳ The human bodies God created — *in His image* — are made to love in this way as well.

- The love of God is so powerful and passionate, it cannot help but be expressed in the creation of new life.

- A man and woman, when they are intimately imaging God's love through their bodies and souls, create this new life as well.

- The sexual embrace of a man and a woman *image the love of God for the world.*

- Anything less is a cheap imitation. Anything less leads us, not closer to God and who He wants us to be, but further away. Sexuality is a *gift.* It is awesome and amazing to think that you and the one to whom you are committed for life can work with God to create new life and can, in a way, be, as a family, an image — a witness — to God's love for the whole world.

> Then the LORD God said, "It is not good that the man should be alone; I will make him a helper fit for him." So out of the ground the LORD God formed every beast of the field and every bird of the air, and brought them to the man to see what he would call them; and whatever the man called every living creature, that was its name. The man gave names to all cattle, and to the birds of the air, and to every beast of the field; but for the man there was not found a helper fit for him. So the LORD God caused a deep sleep to fall upon the man, and while he slept took one of his ribs and closed up its place with flesh; and the rib which the LORD God had taken from the man he made into a woman and brought her to the man. Then the man said,
>
> > "This at last is bone of my bones
> > and flesh of my flesh;

> she shall be called Woman,
>> because she was taken out of man."
>
> Therefore a man leaves his father and his mother and clings to his wife, and they become one flesh. And the man and his wife were both naked, and were not ashamed. (GENESIS 2:18-25)

Now. Can you see how this isn't about rules?

It's not about, "How far can I go before I commit a really, really, really bad sin?"

It's not about, "Oh, man, I'm going to go to hell for this."

Although . . .

It's not about "no." It's about "yes." Very specifically, it's about the "yes" Adam uttered when he saw Eve for the first time. Read it again.

It's all there, in just a few verses. My companion, my friend, my love, the beginnings of family, the great gift of being able to work with God to make new people.

Anything less . . . isn't just not worth it.

It's harmful and in the end . . . kind of sad.

How Far?

The question of "How far can I go?" sexually is pretty common, but you should be seeing that it's the wrong question. There are no rules written down anywhere about how hot is too hot and where your hands should stay away from if you want to avoid sin.

There are no specific rules . . . there is just . . . the rule.

Is this what a disciple of Jesus, committed to the whole truth about who I am, what God put me here for, and what my body's for . . . should be doing?

Jesus is here, right now, with me.

Is this what He wants me to be doing?

Well, let's check on that:

> "You have heard that it was said, 'You shall not commit adultery.' But I say to you that every one who looks at a woman lustfully has already committed adultery with her in his heart." (MATTHEW 5:27)

Yes, Jesus is speaking in the context of adultery here, but it still applies, even if you're not married.

Let's be real. What happens when people lust after one another? What happens when people make out?

They want to go further.

It's *really, really* hard to stop. Like we talked about in the last chapter . . . your body says . . . *keep going.*

I know. This goes totally against the culture. It might even go against the gentle warnings you get from your parents.

But I'm just going to throw it out at you:

Question. Challenge. Think honestly.

???

THIS SURE FEELS GOOD . . . but it is really helping me be the person I know God wants me to be?

Is this a freeing experience, ultimately?

Is this — in any way, shape, or form — an honest kind of experience? Does this have anything to do with love?

I'm not going to tell you what to do.

I just want you to think.

I just want you to pray about it. Pray to *God.*

And listen to what you hear.

> By lust I mean that affection of the mind which aims at the enjoyment of one's self and one's neighbor without reference to God.
>
> — St. Augustine,
> *De Doctrina Christiana,* 3.10

Same-Sex Attraction

THE ANCIENT TRADITION of Christianity, rooted in God's revelation in the Hebrew Scriptures, is that human beings are created male and female, from whose physical and emotional union comes new human life and the bonds of love and family life.

There is a completion and wholeness in the diversity of male and female relationships that is natural and rich.

Being attracted to persons of the same sex, or homosexual attraction, is found across cultures and time. The origins of this attraction in any given individual are mysterious. Most who study it find that there is a combination of physical, emotional and psychological forces at work in a person's struggle. Some individuals with SSA have, indeed, overcome it, but others find it is a lifelong struggle.

Same-sex attraction is not, in itself, a sin. Acting on it is, however. Just like any serious temptation, if we're struggling with same-sex attraction, we absolutely cannot do it alone. We need Jesus to strengthen us through prayer and the sacraments, and we need the help of other people — priests, Catholic counselors — who can help us meet this challenge the way Jesus wants us to.

Porno, Pimping and Ho's

THERE'S A GROWING number of therapists who are very concerned about the impact of pornography — most gotten through the Internet these days — on all of us. They're concerned about the expectations it plants in people's brains and bodies, about the power of addiction.

It's so easy to access pornography now, and you add that to the mainstreaming of the image of prostitution and stripping and you've got a world in which little kids bump and grind and dress up like it's all one big joke.

But is it a joke?

No. It's dehumanizing and creates a culture in which it is even more difficult for men and women to relate to one another as unique human beings, created and loved by God. It sets up a different world entirely, in which human beings are objects that give us pleasure and make us feel powerful. In which women allow themselves to be exploited and put on display for sad, pathetic men who can't do real relationships.

You know in your heart that this isn't the way it's supposed to be. You know that there's no way that using porn or internalizing that brutal attitude to sexuality is going to help you be a good husband or wife or even — if you want to get to the bottom line — a good person.

So separate yourself from it. Be a rebel, be strong. Don't let any of that degraded culture creep into your soul. Take radical action if you need help, if porn has taken hold of you in a way you don't understand — get that help. You won't be sorry you did.

> Let no one deceive you with empty words, for it
> is because of these things that the wrath of God
> comes upon the sons of disobedience. Therefore
> do not associate with them, for once you were
> darkness, but now you are light in the Lord;
> walk as children of light (for the fruit of the
> light is found in all that is good and right and
> true), and try to learn what is pleasing to the
> Lord. Take no part in the unfruitful works of
> darkness, but instead expose them. For it is a
> shame even to speak of the things that they do
> in secret; but when anything is exposed to the
> light it becomes visible, for anything that
> becomes visible is light.
>
> — Ephesians 5:6-13

Contraception

REMEMBER THAT LANGUAGE of the body we talked about a few pages ago? Well, here it comes again.

When a man and a woman give themselves fully to each other, they *give themselves fully to each other.* Their physical intimacy and nakedness speaks a language. It says, "I give my whole self to you, now and forever."

And in our hearts, that's what all of us want. Admit it.

I sincerely doubt that your goal in life is to spend the next sixty years or so engaged in relationship after relationship, disappointment after disappointment.

Your heart yearns for complete acceptance, stability and rock-solid love.

By the way, that yearning, at its root, is a yearning for God, you know. Marriage, as it has been understood by Jewish and Christian

tradition, is an image of that relationship. It echoes, on a human level, the love that God has for us.

Those echoes — it's what all of us who are called to marriage treasure in our hearts as the ideal for ourselves and this long road called life: a relationship that is sure, and trustworthy, in which there is even a sense of "Whatever!" . . . as in "Whatever happens in life . . . whatever God sends our way . . . it's okay! I've got you, you've got me, God has brought us together so we can deal with it and what's more — we can flourish."

And that's the beginning of understanding the ancient Christian teaching that artificial contraception — artificial birth control — is wrong.

Up until the twentieth century, all Christian churches held to this belief. Now it is only the Catholic Church and many Orthodox Christians who still do, although you should know that there is a growing movement in some evangelical groups questioning their own church's acceptance of artificial birth control.

The Catholic Church's teaching on artificial birth control is best expressed in an encyclical (authoritative letter) by Pope Paul VI, written in 1968, called *Humanae Vitae*. Even though it's a papal encyclical and you may say "ew" about the prospect of reading such a thing . . . try it. Look it up. It's on the Vatican website — www.vatican.va — among other places. You might be surprised, forty years after it came out, how . . . prophetic . . . it sounds.

The central points of the Church's teaching on artificial birth control are that sexual intercourse has two main purposes *built into* the act: it is unitive (unifying) and procreative (making babies). To break that, to use our sexuality that purposefully rejects one of those two natural, God-given purposes, is wrong.

Use of artificial birth control distorts our understanding of sexuality. We begin to see children as a problem instead of the natural fruit of love and sexuality. That has a disastrous effect.

And now ... look around you. Think about the role sexuality plays in our culture — in your culture. Why do people say we should be sexually active? To enjoy ourselves. What's the worst thing that can happen in the midst of the play? Oh my gosh — a *baby*. What a disaster!

❓ ❓ ❓

DO YOU SEE how it works? And it *does* work that way. It's the world we live in, a world full of unhappy people trying to find some pleasure, using one another, breaking hearts, and rejecting real love and the joy of an amazing new life.

The Catholic teaching isn't that we shouldn't be responsible in parenting. All women have infertile periods in the midst of every monthly cycle. For most women, keeping track of these periods by way of various natural family planning methods, is a pretty simple way of understanding their bodies and working with God in order to figure out when to bring new life into the world.

But then ... there are always surprises. Maybe you were one.

And was that a ... *bad thing?*

> Jesus ... said to them, "Let the children come to me, do not hinder them; for to such belongs the kingdom of God. Truly, I say to you, whoever does not receive the kingdom of God like a child shall not enter it." And he took them in his arms and blessed them, laying his hands upon them.
>
> — Mark 10:14-16

The Last Word

CHASTITY. Again.

There are lots of other specific issues we could deal with, but I think you've probably got the basic idea:

We're sexual beings. Sexuality is an important element of who we are, and sexual intimacy is a gift from God, an amazing gift that, as Genesis says right from the beginning, is given to us so that we know the joy of self-giving love, echoing God's love as Trinity and God's love for us.

Sexuality can't be separated from the rest of our lives. Yes, it's a powerful force, but we're not fated to give into our desires whenever they overwhelm us.

We just have to think, over and over, every day . . . *who am I?*

Am I a disciple of Jesus?

We just have to think, over and over, every day. . . *what's my life for?*

Is it all about feeling good today, or is it about growing into goodness and joy, and sharing it?

We just have to think, over and over, every day . . . *where are my actions today going to take me?*

Are they taking me closer to God . . . or further away? When I die, what will I have to show God? What will I have done with the gift of life on earth?

What happened to that time, that energy, this body He gave me? Did it all get sucked into a swamp of fantasy, power, and using others . . . or did it actually do a little bit to make the world a better place, to help at least one other person to know how precious he or she is in the eyes of God?

Here's the bottom-line question:

Remember all of those qualities and attitudes we've been talking about? Honesty? Compassion? Real love? Discipleship? Real happiness and joy?

They all still apply. They most *especially* apply when the topic is sexuality. Leaving all that at the door is just not an option for the disciple of Jesus. That's not what we're about. We're about living that

life *all the time*, even when it comes to people we like, whom we want to like us, who we think are cute or hot . . . it all still applies.

All those people — those guys and girls that we're in relationships with — are loved by God, and we *have* to treat them with that same kind of radical, self-giving love that doesn't count the cost and that sees every person as a precious, beloved child of God who deserves . . . love. Not exploitation, not hurt, not a prison of misdirected sexual energy . . . but the freedom of love.

Real freedom.

> When we feel us too bold, remember our own feebleness. When we feel us too faint, remember Christ's strength.
> — St. Thomas More, *Dialogue of Comfort*

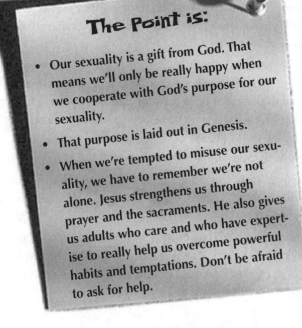

The Point is:

- Our sexuality is a gift from God. That means we'll only be really happy when we cooperate with God's purpose for our sexuality.

- That purpose is laid out in Genesis.

- When we're tempted to misuse our sexuality, we have to remember we're not alone. Jesus strengthens us through prayer and the sacraments. He also gives us adults who care and who have expertise to really help us overcome powerful habits and temptations. Don't be afraid to ask for help.

CHAPTER 9

Whose Life Is Worth Living?

HERE'S THE THING about life:

Once you start drawing lines, all of us are sunk.

THINK ABOUT IT. Think about the lines that you hear drawn here and there about life today. Who's worthy of life? Whose life is worth protecting?

✎ Not brand-new human beings, just fertilized.

✎ Not unborn babies.

✎ Not the severely disabled.

✎ Not the terminally ill.

✎ Not the elderly, who need a lot of care.

Hmm. I'm thinking . . . at one point or another, I might fit into a couple of those categories.

You too.

Feeling nervous yet?

"I Formed You"

THE QUESTION-OF-LIFE ISSUES can be complicated, and there are many different sub-issues we could consider. We'll touch on a few of them.

But as was the case with sexuality, the most important thing is to get our principles straight and true, right now. Once you do that, everything else falls into place.

With life issues, the principle is this:

God is the creator of life. He gives life to each person, as a gift.

It is always morally wrong to deliberately and directly end a human life.

Always.

We just don't have that right.

We don't have the right to kill children in the womb. We don't have the right to neglect those who can't care for themselves. We don't have the right to genetically manipulate newly conceived human beings in a petri dish.

This is not the way of a disciple of Jesus.

You can get distracted by talk about "rights" and "choices" and even "progress" all you want, but every time, you have to come back to this:

- What would Jesus' response to the pregnant woman or girl be?
- What would Jesus' response to the very sick person be?
- What is Jesus' response to the distressed and the helpless?
- What is Jesus' response to the tiny small person created in a laboratory?
- Is it *ever* — "Let's kill you and move on"?
- Is it *ever* — "Let's experiment on you, okay"?
- Is it *ever* — "Your life isn't worth living. You're better off dead"?

???

No.

This answer puts us in difficult situations in which much is required of us. In which we have to admit to wrongdoing, in which we have to accept responsibility, in which we have to sacrifice our personal desires, in which we have to work very, very hard in distressing situations.

By now, you should know the answer to *that*.

Not in words, but in action, right? Hanging on the cross, Jesus speaks loud and clear:

Every person is worth profound, sacrificial love.

Suffering happens.

I'm with you when it does.

> "Truly, I say to you, as you did it to one of the least of these my brethren, you did it to me."
> — Matthew 25:40

Abortion

ABORTION IS NOT A NEW THING, invented a few decades ago. Ancient cultures knew all about abortion. And just in case you think that this means it's okay, since, you know . . . everyone's done it, well, think again.

Those same ancient cultures — most of them — also practiced some sort of infanticide, exposing infants to death after they were born if they seemed weak or were disabled or were . . . girls.

Is that okay?

Of course not. The point is, the ancients knew abortion, and this was the world — of the brutal Roman Empire — in which Christianity came.

And from the very beginning, Christians, disciples of Jesus, spoke out against abortion. Take a look at this document, called the *Didache*, which dates from the early second century. It's a collection of Christian teachings:

> 1. There are two ways, one of life and one of death; and between the two ways there is a great difference.
>
> 2. Now, this is the way of life: . . .
>
> The second commandment of the Teaching: "Do not murder; do not commit adultery"; do not corrupt boys; do not fornicate; "do not steal"; do not practice magic; do not go in for sorcery; *do not murder a child by abortion or kill a newborn infant.* "Do not covet your neighbor's property; do not commit perjury; do not bear false witness"; do not slander; do not bear grudges. Do not be double-minded or double-tongued, for a double tongue is "a deadly snare." Your words shall not be dishonest or hollow, but substantiated by action. Do not be greedy or extortionate or hypocritical or malicious or arrogant. Do not plot against your neighbor. Do not hate anybody; but

reprove some, pray for others, and still others love more
than your own life [emphasis mine].

In fact, when you compare how Christians lived and valued life
in the earliest days, you can't help but see this amazing contrast
between the Way of Jesus' disciples and the broader culture of the
Roman Empire. In the world of the first century, children were regularly exploited in every way, including sexually. Abortion and
infanticide were common ways of dealing with unwanted preg-
nancies and "unfit" babies.

Christians were notable — were even *weird* — for standing up
against these practices. But they just knew — this is not the way of
a disciple.

If God loved this person into existence — who are we to take
that life? Did God just create this person and then step back, saying
to us, "Sure, go ahead. Kill."

Impossible.

NOTHING'S CHANGED in two thousand years. No matter what the circumstances, it is never moral to abort an unborn child. Of course,
in the United States it is certainly *legal* to abort an unborn child, but
that doesn't make it moral.

Not that this is easy when it happens to you. Even if you think
you've got your morals fully formed, if an unexpected pregnancy
happens to you or someone you care about, the temptation is very,
very strong to spend a few hundred dollars to make it all go away
so life can go on as planned.

Trouble is, life doesn't go on as planned. An unexpected pregnancy changes life, no matter how someone ends up dealing with
it. Nothing is ever the same, and a girl or woman who agrees to
abort her child lives with that for the rest of her life — every

anniversary of the abortion, every anniversary of the due date . . . for the rest of her life.

Read the stories of women who've had abortions and, by the grace of God, found the merciful forgiveness of Jesus. Read about their pain and suffering and regret.

Then tell me that abortion will bring everything back to normal.

The point is, any "choice" you make in an unexpected pregnancy brings with it some suffering:

Keeping the baby to raise yourself: the normal wear and tear of pregnancy and parenthood; adjusting goals; social awkwardness.

Placing the baby for adoption: the difficulties of pregnancy; embarrassment; the pain of saying good-bye to the baby, even out of love.

Aborting the baby: bearing the truth that your choice ended an innocent, helpless human life who didn't ask to be conceived.

The question we have to ask ourselves with this — as with any moral choice — is: Which is the most loving choice? The most *truly* loving choice for all. That's it. Period.

Which is why it's so important to keep the truth of that cross in our heads: Love involves suffering and sacrifice. You can't escape it, you can't run away, and the more you try, the harder it will come back to you, when it does come back — eventually.

The challenge of discipleship isn't to be a martyr and run after suffering. That's not what Jesus did. The challenge is to love, and if loving involves sacrifice and suffering, to accept it, as Jesus did, knowing that Jesus is with you and understands.

This isn't an issue that is distant to us. People we know and love have had abortions and, despite our best efforts, may in the future. We may be tempted to have an abortion ourselves or to pressure someone else into it.

This is not a "they" issue. It's a "we" issue because we are all God's children; as Christians, we are all the Body of Christ, and the suffering of any part of that Body is *our* suffering.

So for that reason, when it comes to the issue of abortion, we have to be so very closely connected to Jesus for strength. We have to teach ourselves, continually, about the preciousness of each human life, of the truth that God doesn't bring life into existence so we can snuff it out.

But I feel that the greatest destroyer of peace today is abortion, because it is a war against the child, a direct killing of the innocent child, murder by the mother herself. And if we accept that a mother can kill even her own child, how can we tell other people not to kill one another? How do we persuade a woman not to have an abortion? As always, we must persuade her with love and we remind ourselves that love means to be willing to give until it hurts. Jesus gave even His life to love us. So, the mother who is thinking of abortion, should be helped to love, that is, to give until it hurts her plans, or her free time, to respect the life of her child. The father of that child, whoever he is, must also give until it hurts.

By abortion, the mother does not learn to love, but kills even her own child to solve her problems. And, by abortion, that father is told that he does not have to take any responsibility at all for the child he has brought into the world. The father is likely to put other women into the same trouble. So abortion just leads to more abortion. Any country that accepts abortion is not teaching its people to love, but to use any violence to get what they want. This is why the greatest destroyer of love and peace is abortion.

— MOTHER TERESA,
NATIONAL PRAYER BREAKFAST, 1997

The End

BACK IN THE DAY, back a long time ago, one of the things Christians were encouraged to think about was the "Happy Death."

Sounds weird. Sounds impossible.

But you know what? Death is a part of life. Not any of us will avoid the end to our earthly existence. For Christians, too, death plays a sort of important role in our thinking — we are, as disciples of Jesus, called not to be afraid of death any longer because Jesus has conquered it:

> "Death is swallowed up in victory."
> "O death, where is your victory?
> O death, where is your sting?"
>
> The sting of death is sin, and the power of sin is the law. But thanks be to God, who gives us the victory through our Lord Jesus Christ. (1 Corinthians 15:54-57)

The "happy death" involved knowing and believing in Jesus' power over death, and it also involved being spiritually prepared for death and being surrounded by people who loved and cared for you, who would accompany you to that door as far as they could go, praying and singing and holding you . . . and praying for you after you went through.

The "happy death."

A sad moment, but a natural one, and one which is now drenched in hope because Jesus lives, and so will we, if we are part of His Body — that *Risen* Body, remember?

So when Christians think about physical suffering and the threat of death, we are never and have never been a "physical existence at all costs" kind of people. That truth we keep coming to still applies — God is the author of life, God is the only one with the power to give and take life.

So when death is imminent . . . it is time to let go.

But, when death is imminent . . . it is not time to cause it.

Ever.

The ancient Catholic teaching on end-of-life issues has always involved balancing these two truths:

We don't have the right to deliberately take a life.

We don't want to artificially and unnecessarily prolong the process of dying, either.

A *happy, peaceful,* and *natural* passage to eternal life is the hope of all Christians. Catholic teaching on the end of life embodies it.

This whole end-of-life business may seem far away from you, but it isn't. Chances are your family has already been through this, and if it hasn't . . . it's coming. These are decisions you'll have to make, at some point, some day. So just like with every other moral issue, it's important to understand the right moral stance, develop and nurture it in little ways, and prepare for the moments when the big decisions will be yours to make.

Means Test

IN CATHOLIC THINKING about the end of life and serious illness, you're going to hear about distinctions between "ordinary" and "extraordinary" means of treatment. Morally, we're obligated to provide ordinary means of treatment to the ill, but the provision of extraordinary means isn't obligated.

The tricky part is, of course, that as technology advances, the definition of "extraordinary means" shifts. A respirator might have been extraordinary means a half-century ago, but in most cases, it's considered "ordinary" means today.

One other important point: Care — this is providing water and food — even if that food and water is through tubes or in the form of little sips — isn't treatment. It's care. It's what human beings need and deserve to keep living, and we always owe that to the weak, the dying and the disabled.

Help

"EUTHANASIA" IS A TERM that's used quite a bit, but it's important to understand what it is and what it is not. Euthanasia refers to directly causing the death of another who is ill or dying, either by stopping ordinary treatment or care, or killing that person with medications.

Euthanasia is immoral, because directly ending a human life is always immoral.

Let the *Catechism of the Catholic Church* take it:

> Discontinuing medical procedures that are burdensome, dangerous, extraordinary, or disproportionate to the expected outcome can be legitimate; it is the refusal of "over-zealous" treatment. Here one does not will to cause death; one's inability to impede it is merely accepted. The decisions should be made by the patient if he is competent and able or, if not, by those legally entitled to act for the patient, whose reasonable will and legitimate interests must always be respected.   — CCC, 2278

> Even if death is thought imminent, the ordinary care owed to a sick person cannot be legitimately interrupted. The use of painkillers to alleviate the sufferings of the dying, even at the risk of shortening their days, can be morally in conformity with human dignity if death is not willed as either an end or a means, but only foreseen and tolerated as inevitable. Palliative care is a special form of disinterested charity. As such it should be encouraged.   — CCC, 2279

A lot of proponents of euthanasia of various forms say it's moral because it ends suffering. There are a lot of problems with that:

- Suffering is a part of life, even terrible suffering. We don't seek it, we want suffering to end — *God* wants suffering to end — but killing a person is not acceptable.

- Take that to its logical conclusion. It sounds kind of nice — feeding a suffering person some drugs to "end their pain." But why the pills? Why not suffocate someone or shoot them? Their suffering would be ended, right?

- I'll bet you recoil from that idea, don't you? Think about that. Think about your reaction. It tells you something about the intrinsic immorality of ending a life, an immorality that the nice image and language of pills somehow manages to hide.

- Our call is not to deliberately kill, but to accompany people and minister to them in their suffering.

- Again, the question of Jesus comes up. Confronted with the suffering person, what do you think Jesus calls us to do? Kill? Or have compassion . . . to *suffer with.*

- Remember: If there are extraordinary means being used to *prolong the dying process* (not "keep someone alive") . . . it is fine to discontinue those extraordinary means.

Be Real

WHEN IT COMES TO end-of-life issues, we have to be brutally real. It's horrible and painful to think about, but there is another important reason that we, as disciples, have to be strong in our stand against direct killing.

It's because the pressures *to* kill are great.

None of these cases of dying people happen in a vacuum, and many of them happen in circumstances that are less than ideal: in which family members harbor grudges; in which family members have their own lives to get back to; in which finances are an issue; in which governments and hospitals and clinics look at the dying, not as human beings, but as names on a list that are costing them a lot of money.

Life in a Lab

ONE OF THE MOST PRESSING issues that we're confronting today is that of really young human beings and how we should treat them.

In short: Are young human embryos lab rats? Should scientists be free to experiment on them, clone them, and then get rid of them?

Short answer: No.

There are folks who argue strenuously that we should be able to do just that. When you're confronted with these arguments, step up and ask some radical, tough questions:

- Why is this okay? Who decided it's okay and why?
- How do you draw the line? If it's okay to experiment on a seven-day-old embryo, why not an eight-day-old embryo? Or a fourteen-day-old embryo? Or a month-old preborn human being? (Answer — there's no way. Just as in abortion, all of these lines are arbitrarily drawn. The only way to guarantee the protection of all human life is to draw the line where God, through nature, draws it — at conception. There's your new human being. Don't mess with it.)
- Who's benefiting financially from this?

???

EVERY HUMAN LIFE began as a fertilized egg, then moved on through the various stages of division and development. *You* began that way. The Church holds firm to the truth that it's wrong for human beings to try to play God at any stage of life — beginning or end:

> *For you formed my inward parts; you knitted me together in my mother's womb.*

I praise you, for I am wonderfully made. Wonderful are your works! You know me right well; my frame was not hidden from you, when I was being made in secret, intricately wrought in the depths of the earth.

Your eyes beheld my unformed substance; in your book were written, everyone of them, the days that were formed for me, when as yet there was none of them.
(PSALM 139: 13-16)

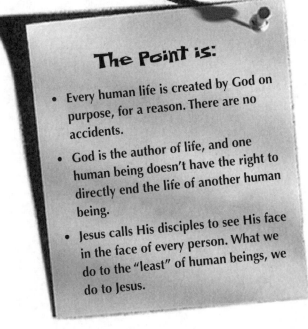

The Point is:

- Every human life is created by God on purpose, for a reason. There are no accidents.

- God is the author of life, and one human being doesn't have the right to directly end the life of another human being.

- Jesus calls His disciples to see His face in the face of every person. What we do to the "least" of human beings, we do to Jesus.

CHAPTER 10

It's a Big World With Too Many Problems. Can't I Just Live My Own Life?

WE'VE TALKED A LOT about you in this book.

Your conscience, your virtues, your holiness, your capacity for (gulp) sanctity.

You're great.

But you're not alone in that greatness.

There are scores, scads, tons, millions of other great "you's" in the world.

In fact — every person. Every single person who's walking on this earth is a "you" — created and loved by God. A "you" who is a person of dignity and who has God-given rights.

So?

What's that got to do with the "you" right here and now, reading this book?

Everything.

> Is such the fast that I choose, a day for a man to humble himself? Is it to bow down his head like a rush, and to spread sackcloth and ashes under him? Will you call this a fast, and a day acceptable to the LORD? Is not this the fast that I choose: to loose the bonds of wickedness, to undo the thongs of the yoke, to let the

It's a Big World With Too Many Problems.
Can't I Just Live My Own Life?

111

oppressed go free, and to break every yoke? Is it not to share your bread with the hungry, and bring the homeless poor into your house; when you see the naked, to cover him, and not to hide yourself from your own flesh?

— Isaiah 58:5-7

Love and Sacrifice

I HOPE YOU'VE NOTICED that the theme of this book about you and the life God calls you to live hasn't been about rules.

It's simply been about who we are as human beings, created by God in His image. Our road to happiness now and forever is the road that God has laid out in front of us, with the map built within us and given to us through Scripture and the Church. That road is marked by love and sacrifice.

Sacrifice when we have the choice whether or not to help a classmate.

Love when we have the choice whether or not to be kind.

Sacrifice when we have the choice of how to best use our time.

Love — real love — when we have the choice of how to be in a relationship.

???

ALL THAT'S TRUE.

Here's something else that's true:

That stance of love and sacrifice, the practice of all those virtues — doesn't stop with the people you see every day, the people you know and who are your friends and live in your neighborhood.

Jesus' disciples have *always* understood that the call to love takes in everyone, that we are obligated to see to the well-being of all those in need, not just those conveniently nearby.

There are two ways of answering the call, ways that are related and intersect, but that should both play a role in the life of a disciple of Jesus.

Justice

JUSTICE IS THE IDEA that all human persons deserve their "due" — what they deserve because they are human beings: life, food, shelter, medical care, work, religious freedom, and fair treatment are the basics.

The Church has a whole body of teaching on justice — the social teaching of the Church helps us see how the economic, governmental, and social structures of communities and nations can be shaped so that basic human dignity and rights are supported. The Catholic Church has representatives involved in many international organizations, such as the United Nations, to keep the voice for human dignity alive.

All of us are encouraged to do what we can to live out the social teaching of the Church, as well. We can vote (once we're old enough), we can lobby, we can raise awareness, and we can choose career paths that are dedicated to shaping those structures, too.

It's a **Big World** With Too Many Problems.
Can't I Just Live My Own Life?

It all comes down to this:

> *Hear this, you who trample upon the needy, and bring the*
> *poor of the land to an end, saying, "When will the new*
> *moon be over, that we may sell grain? And the sabbath,*
> *that we may offer wheat for sale, that we may make the*
> *ephah small and the shekel great, and deal deceitfully with*
> *false balances, that we may buy the poor for silver and the*
> *needy for a pair of sandals, and sell the refuse of the*
> *wheat.?" The Lord has sworn by the pride of Jacob: "Surely*
> *I will never forget any of their deeds."* (AMOS 8:4-7)

Get that? This is nothing new or politically trendy. Those words
— *God's* words — are from the Old Testament, written a few centuries even before Jesus came to earth. You want to talk about sin?
A world in which the wealthy nations waste amazing amounts of
food every day at the same time millions are starving: sin. A world
in which people pay thousands of dollars for medication for domes-
tic pets and for plastic surgery and in which thousands of children
die every day from a lack of basic vaccinations and medical care:
sin.

CHARITY IS THE CALL for us to directly help people in need, whether
they are near or far. The command to directly care for the needy is
all over the Bible:

> *"You shall not pervert the justice due to the sojourner or*
> *to the fatherless; or take a widow's garment in pledge; but*
> *you shall remember that you were a slave in Egypt and*
> *the LORD your God redeemed you from there; therefore I*
> *command you to do this.*
> *"When you reap your harvest in your field, and have*
> *forgotten a sheaf in the field, you shall not go back to get*

it; it shall be for the sojourner, the fatherless, and the widow; that the Lord your God may bless you in all the work of your hands. When you beat your olive trees, you shall not go over the boughs again; it shall be for the sojourner, the fatherless, and the widow. When you gather the grapes of your vineyard, you shall not glean it afterward; it shall be for the sojourner, the fatherless, and the widow. You shall remember that you were a slave in the land of Egypt; therefore I command you to do this." (DEUTERONOMY 24:17-22)

Jesus reveals even more to us and deepens what God had revealed to the Jewish people. Jesus makes it all even more personal:

"When the Son of Man comes in his glory, and all the angels with him, then he will sit on his glorious throne. Before him will be gathered all the nations, and he will separate them one from another as a shepherd separates the sheep from the goats, and he will place the sheep at his right hand, but the goats at the left. Then the King will say to those at his right hand, 'Come, O blessed of my Father, inherit the kingdom prepared for you from the foundation of the world; for I was hungry and you gave me food, I was thirsty and you gave me drink, I was a stranger and you welcomed me, I was naked and you clothed me, I was sick and you visited me, I was in prison and you came to me.' Then the righteous will answer him, 'Lord, when did we see you hungry and feed you, or thirsty and give you drink? And when did we see you a stranger and welcome you, or naked and clothe you? And when did we see you sick or in prison and visit you?' And the King will answer them, 'Truly, I say to you, as you did it to one of the least of these, you did it to me.'" (MATTHEW 25:31-40)

115

It's a Big World With Too Many Problems. Can't I Just Live My Own Life?

That's a lot of Scripture there, but really, it's all we need to know. Read it all again, think about it, and pray for a minute. What would life be like if we lived that way? How would the world be different if we made our choices mindful of the call to justice and charity?

The Christian is called to both, and to do both out of love.

It's a busy life we're called to lead, isn't it?

Well, just remember, Jesus doesn't call us to go hunting out problems or solving all the world's issues. He invites us to "follow Him" from where we are. That's the place to start — where you sit right this minute.

No, it's not that we're to invent challenges — but to meet those that are right here, in front of us, in any small way we can.

No one ever died regretting that they helped other people *too much* during their lives.

In fact . . . it just might be the opposite.

When we think about "justice," some current issues that come to mind are:

War and Peace

What about war?

God wants peace. He created a world at peace, and in the fulfillment of His kingdom, that's what will reign: peace (see Isaiah 2:4; 65:17-25).

But, tragically, we live in a world still filled with sin. Some people try to harm others. When all other ways of trying to protect the weak from those trying to harm them through violence have failed, it is permissible to use force — not to gain power, but to protect. It's what has come to be known as "just war."

The idea of a "just war" was developed over centuries by Christian thinkers from St. Augustine in the fourth century to St. Thomas Aquinas in the thirteenth, to now. In the present day, the conversa-

AMY WELBORN

tion that theologians have about just war is different than it was in the fourth century and continues to develop.

The weapons we have available are far more destructive than anything ancient peoples could have imagined. Questions about the responsibility of nations to bring justice by force to nations that don't directly threaten them have arisen over the past ten years.

Where does a nation's responsibility begin and end? Is there a risk of nations trying to do too much and even embracing an inappropriate role as near-messiahs? The reality of terrorism also necessitates new thinking about use of force.

Throughout that conversation, the essence of the teaching on just war remains the same. In order for a war to be considered "just," several standards have to be met:

- An aggressor is threatening with certain and grave harm.
- All other means of protection have been exhausted.
- There must be a reasonable hope of success.
- The use of arms can't produce evils more serious than what's being fought against — massive destruction and killing of innocent people, for example.

War is always tragic, and all of us have a responsibility to work for peace in our own lives and in our world.

Capital Punishment

WHEN WE HEAR of a terrible crime committed, our instincts and emotions often lead us to believe that the best response is to take the life of the criminal as well.

Indeed, for much of human history, the death penalty has been a very common way of punishing criminals guilty of the most terrible crimes.

The Catholic Church teaches that a government does, indeed, have the right to punish criminals in this way. It's an expression of

It's a Big World With Too Many Problems.
Can't I Just Live My Own Life?

the idea of self-defense. As tragic as it always is to take a human life, if that happens as a part of the act of self-defense or protecting the weak, it can be justified.

But, as the *Catechism of the Catholic Church* points out, times are changing. Capital punishment was commonly used in eras and cultures in which it was more difficult to assure that a dangerous person would, indeed, stay locked up securely. In the world today, that is simply no longer the case. It is very possible and not a challenge for a government to imprison a dangerous, unrepentant criminal for the rest of his natural life. In addition, this kind of punishment leaves more possibility for conversion and redemption.

Economic Inequality

Economics is complicated. When entire groups of people in various countries are impoverished, malnourished, suffering and starving, it's not for simple reasons, nor are those problems solved by simple means such as, "Let's just give them stuff." We *need* to give them stuff, but the fact is, our goal as citizens of this planet, as brothers and sisters of those in perpetual need, should be to help, in any way we can, construction of societies where there is no longer any kind of massive, grinding poverty or extreme inequalities.

The Catholic Church is the Church of the poor, and always has been. The saints are, for the most part, people who have given their lives in service to Jesus through the poor. It's an awareness we need to cultivate ourselves, every day, as we grow in holiness.

Part of that is cultivating another kind of awareness — of this injustice. We're each just a tiny cog in a huge global machine, but the plight of the poor, the voice of Jesus in the poor, demands awareness and, when we can, some kind of help — both in terms of charity and justice. There is a deep and broad understanding in our Catholic tradition that the earth is not ours — it is the Lord's. What we have is a gift, and it is, well — *sinful* for some to have too much while others have nothing. It's not what God wants. It's not the way God created the world to be.

> If you have money, consider that perhaps the only reason God allowed it to fall into your hands was in order that you might find joy and perfection by throwing it away.
>
> — Thomas Merton, *Seeds of Contemplation*

So what can we do? Be educated. Consider using our talents, as we select a career, in a way that contributes to economic justice, not greater injustice. Make our choices about what we buy, what we eat and what we wear reflective of that reality. That what we have is a gift, and those who suffer around the world, and could be helped by us, are not numbers or ideas. They are people. They are *Jesus*.

The Environment

REMEMBER GENESIS?

Remember how it starts?

Creation — that's it. What they call the "environment."

It has been at the center of Judeo-Christian faith since the beginning — the firm belief that God's creation is good and beautiful, and that our role in the context of that creation is to be a good steward — to care for it. It's right there:

> And God blessed them, and God said to them, "Be fruitful and multiply, and fill the earth and subdue it; and have dominion over the fish of the sea and over the birds of the air and over every living thing that moves upon the earth. . . ." And God saw everything that he had made, and behold, it was very good. And there was evening and there was morning, a sixth day. (GENESIS 1:28, 31)

Environmental concerns are huge right now, and it's something Christians are and should be concerned about. As the *Catechism of the Catholic Church* says:

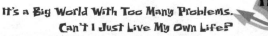

> Each creature possesses its own particular goodness and
> perfection. . . . Each of the various creatures, willed in its
> own being, reflects in its own way a ray of God's infinite
> wisdom and goodness. Man must therefore respect the
> particular goodness of every creature, to avoid any dis-
> ordered use of things which would be in contempt of the
> Creator and would bring disastrous consequences for
> human beings and their environment.   — CCC, 339

However, as Christians, we need to be wary of some traps out there. Environmentalism, as a movement, has some flaws. For some, it's almost a religion in itself. So keep this in mind as you get involved and learn more:

- Watch the science. Don't assume that what one group says about a certain problem is true without getting the other side.
- Keep your perspective. Cities in the West are *far* cleaner than they were, say a hundred and fifty years ago in the beginnings of the Industrial Revolution. Lakes and other bodies of water in the United States are even cleaner than they were *forty* years ago. Get the whole picture before you get alarmed.
- Most importantly: There's a strain in modern environmental movements that basically sees human beings as the enemy. The world, they say, would be a lot better off without human beings. Human beings are a problem. *But that's not Christian.* It doesn't even make sense.

There are strong reasons for disciples of Jesus to be concerned about the environment, to conserve, protect, and recycle. God gave us the earth to love and treasure, not to destroy.

But watch out... the earth isn't God. Only God is God. And human beings — each of whom is precious and wonderful — aren't problems. They're people. God wants people to be here. He likes them.

Justice, Charity, and Love

THERE'S NO "EITHER-OR" for Jesus' disciples.

We're not asked to choose between caring about global economic, political, and social structures that condemn millions to poverty around the world *or* between directly helping those people with charitable donations.

Human beings suffer for complex and innumerable reasons. Some of those reasons are structural, and some are personal — people can't be bothered to help.

Disciples of Jesus — you and me — don't choose justice or charity. We choose both. No, we can't do everything, but when you look at the saints across history, you find them meeting Jesus in the poor in all kinds of different ways: through direct encounters with the poor, as well as through leadership and efforts to change.

The challenge, though, is to never forget that the "poor" aren't symbols or numbers. They are *people*. To get all swept up in "issues" and advocacy, while neglecting the real good you could do for Christ in the poor, the sick, the immigrant, the elderly, the unborn, the pregnant teens, the imprisoned — *right in your own town . . .* that's not the call of Jesus.

Pope Benedict helps us see this clearly in his encyclical *Deus Caritas Est* ("God Is Love") in which he pulls all of this together and reminds us about the "Christ" at the center of a Christian's concern for justice and charity:

> Love of neighbor is thus shown to be possible in the way proclaimed by the Bible, by Jesus. It consists in the very fact that, in God and with God, I love even the person whom I do not like or even know. This can only take place on the basis of an intimate encounter with God, an encounter which has become a communion of will, even affecting my feelings. Then I learn to look on this other person not simply with my eyes and my feelings, but

It's a Big World With Too Many Problems.
Can't I Just Live My Own Life?

121

from the perspective of Jesus Christ. His friend is my friend. Going beyond exterior appearances, I perceive in others an interior desire for a sign of love, of concern. This I can offer them not only through the organizations intended for such purposes, accepting it perhaps as a political necessity. Seeing with the eyes of Christ, I can give to others much more than their outward necessities; I can give them the look of love which they crave.

— *Deus Caritas Est*, 18

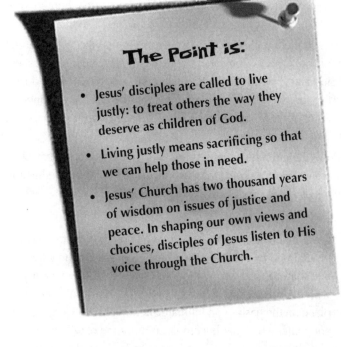

The Point is:

- Jesus' disciples are called to live justly: to treat others the way they deserve as children of God.

- Living justly means sacrificing so that we can help those in need.

- Jesus' Church has two thousand years of wisdom on issues of justice and peace. In shaping our own views and choices, disciples of Jesus listen to His voice through the Church.

"Be Not Afraid."

LIFE IS CHALLENGING. It is also mysterious, confusing, hard, and uncertain.

But most of all, life is *wonderful*.

This life that God gave you because He loves you so much you just have to exist is wonderful because it is just full of wonder. Or it should be.

In the end, that's what this whole book has been about: inviting you to see how wonderful your life *is* and how wonderful it *can be*.

When you think about all the advice and teaching you've received about "how to live your life" over the past few years, you might find yourself at times wanting to close your eyes and block your ears and yell, "Stop! I'll do it my way — I can figure it out!"

Please don't.

I hope you've seen that the wisdom you've picked up — the real wisdom — wasn't dreamed up yesterday. And I hope you've figured out that if this wisdom about honesty, integrity, faithfulness, and simply being a good person had consistently made people miserable through the centuries . . . it wouldn't be considered wisdom anymore.

Going even deeper, I hope that you've seen that if this Way — the Way of the disciples of Jesus that is about radical, self-giving love — didn't bring people joy — it would have died out a long time ago.

In the end, it all comes down to this:

↳ God made you because He loves you and has a purpose for you.

↪ He made every other person out of love and with a purpose, too.

↪ The moral life is about living with both of those truths in mind all the time.

↪ The world is broken because of sin — because so many of us forget to hold those first two truths in balance.

↪ God came to earth as the Word made flesh — Jesus — to reconcile the world to Him. Death no longer has power, and neither does sin.

↪ The way to real happiness, now and forever, is being true to the self God made us to be and being in union with Him through Jesus.

The Church is where we find Jesus.

This journey *is* a journey. When you read what the saints — people we know who were holy and close to Jesus — said about their own journeys, you can really understand that. All of them knew that they would never be finished until they were finally with God in heaven.

Please don't look at your life, as a disciple of Jesus — as one more competition, contest, or achievement. It is not that at all. Don't read through this book and make a checklist of things to do and things to be or stages to achieve.

It's not about working harder or racking up points.

It's about loving more fiercely and faithfully. It's about pouring ourselves out in love: the love of Jesus that fills us, that we, then, share. Radically. Shockingly. Joyfully.

Real, true, authentic love.

It's what you want. It's what we all want. And we want it for a reason — we were *created* to want it, because God is love. *Deus Caritas Est.*

Can you love like that . . . for the next minute?

And then for another minute?

And for one more?

Do you want to know how? And what happens when we do? Listen to Pope Benedict's homily from Midnight Mass, Christmas, 2006:

"Yet now further questions arise: how are we to love God with all our mind, when our intellect can barely reach him? How are we to love him with all our heart and soul, when our heart can only catch a glimpse of him from afar, when there are so many contradictions in the world that would hide his face from us? This is where the two ways in which God has 'abbreviated' his Word come together. He is no longer distant. He is no longer unknown. He is no longer beyond the reach of our heart. He has become a child for us, and in so doing he has dispelled all doubt. He has become our neighbor, restoring in this way the image of man, whom we often find so hard to love. For us, God has become a gift. He has given himself. He has entered time for us. He who is the Eternal One, above time; he has assumed our time and raised it to himself on high. Christmas has become the Feast of gifts in imitation of God who has given himself to us. Let us allow our heart, our soul and our mind to be touched by this fact! Among the many gifts that we buy and receive, let us not forget the true gift: to give each other something of ourselves, to give each other something of our time, to open our time to God. In this way anxiety disappears, joy is born, and the feast is created."

About that feast. . .

You know you're invited, right?

Are you coming?

Be not afraid!
— Pope John Paul II

For Further Reading

Confessions, St. Augustine

The Imitation of Christ, Thomas à Kempis

Introduction to the Devout Life, St. Francis de Sales

The Story of a Soul, St. Thérèse of Lisieux

The Seven-Storey Mountain, Thomas Merton

The Long Loneliness, Dorothy Day

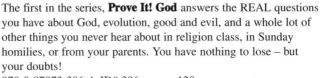

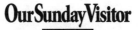